Clean Your House Like A Pro

Proven Methods to Keep Your Home Organized, Deep Clean
All Your Rooms and Tidy Up Your House

By

Grace Burke

While every precaution has been taken in the preparation of this book, the publisher assumes no responsibility for errors or omissions, or for damages resulting from the use of the information contained herein.

This book is for entertainment and informational purposes only. The views expressed are those of the author alone and should not be taken as expert instruction or commands. The reader is responsible for his or her own actions. Neither the author nor the publisher assumes any responsibility or liability whatsoever on behalf of the purchaser or reader of these materials. The reader is responsible for their own use of any products or methods mentioned in this publication.

This book includes information about products and equipment offered by third parties. As such, the author does not assume responsibility or liability for any third party products or opinions. Third party product manufacturers have not sanctioned this book, nor does the author receive any compensation from said manufacturers for sharing information regarding their products.

CLEAN YOUR HOUSE LIKE A PRO
First edition. December 12, 2019.
Copyright © 2019 Grace Burke.

Print ISBN: 978-1-64786-208-4

Table of Contents

Introduction

Welcome! If you picked up this book, you've most likely reached a dilemma with your cleaning habits. If you looked up from this introduction and scanned the room you're in, you might see piles of clothes, a collection of fur building up in the corner, and perhaps a layer of grime on your closest window. You mentally take note that the windows need a good cleaning and start to rack your brain for the date you last cleaned them. You may even get up the nerve to clean them all in the morning (if on a Saturday). You spend 3 hours getting them crystal clear and turn around to see the dozens of other surfaces in dire need of attention.

If any of that sounds familiar, you're in the right place. This book is for everyone who dreams of a clean, functional home and has found one roadblock after another trying to get to that point. It's here to take the burdens of housekeeping off you and help you grow to appreciate the routine of cleaning. It takes the guesswork out of the effectiveness of different cleaning products by providing its own set of test results. It gathers the massive bulk of cleaning tasks and breaks them down in a way that returns your weekends to you. More importantly, it's here to eliminate your frustrations over the planning and execution of cleaning tasks so you can focus on more important things in your life.

Before now, you may have felt the only hope your home had for a clean start required gathering your closest friends to help you scrub from top to bottom. It was certainly how I felt when faced with a 3,000 square foot home with several cats, my own full-time job, a ninety minute commute, and a studio-size vacation rental to manage.

I was no stranger to cleaning when I inherited my home and added my lifestyle to it. I have been cleaning houses since high school and had seen everything from abandoned homes with mystery stains on floors to new construction high-rise apartments in need of a simple dusting. I found cleaning others' homes to be soothing and felt they granted me a sense of accomplishment when I finished. I curated my own set of supplies including a treasured vacuum that worked so well, carpets looked brand new. I enjoyed sharing my knowledge of how to clean an antique cast iron tub and what to do with soap scum building up on acrylic shower walls.

I relied on this experience heavily to find my routine in my new home. Like anyone, I craved the fresh start that comes with a completely spotless home. If I was going to find that fresh start, however, I was going to have to confront my schedule. I was knee deep in vacation rental bookings, long days at the office, keeping cats well cared for, and the little bit of time carved out just to breathe. It didn't happen overnight, but I took my house from an allergy bomb to ready for guests at any hour. The difference was extraordinary. I no longer felt like every weekend was dedicated to scrubbing top to bottom to turn over the vacation rental. I found there were nights that I finally had nothing to do in the way of housework and those began to stack up.

I found not only savings in my time after implementing my cleaning method, but a savings in money, too. Every ad on social media for cleaning product delivery services called to me. I had a host of new items and surfaces to keep clean that my old arsenal of products couldn't cover. I had to expand my collection and that meant testing (aka spending money) on new products. Once I found what worked, along with a few homemade alternatives that cost pennies on the dollar, my spending went way down. I was able to clean more surfaces, more often, and for less money.

I also found that the deep cleaning and subsequent maintenance cleaning protected furniture and fixtures from premature aging. I saw this in action when I visited a friend who had installed a vanity sink in their bathroom less than 6 months prior. It wasn't top shelf quality, but I could see how the buildup of dirt around the faucet had actually started eating away at the shiny metallic surface. It hadn't even been a year and the several hundred dollar vanity needed a new faucet! I was tempted in that moment to rush home and check every fixture for signs of deterioration. I restrained, but I could not forget one of the greatest benefits of cleaning- - the money saved on costly repairs, frequent upgrades, and new items that come from neglecting what you currently own.

I'm familiar with my own sense of accomplishment after performing even the most mundane task of loading the dishwasher. But there's actual evidence from studies that show a positive relationship between mental health and a clean home. Originally published in 2008, a UCLA study in the Personality and Social Psychology bulletin looks at 60 dual-income spouses to find whether time spent at home is restful or detracting. What they found is that in homes with unfinished projects or tasks left undone, there were more negative associations with living there. In homes where cleanliness reigned, study participants reported being happier while occupying their home. Even in a small case study like this, those results are powerful. I want that sense of restfulness and relaxation for everyone who reads this book. Not just for the dual-income households who may have hired cleaning services. Anyone can find the serenity that comes from a clean home and this book is here to help.

Now that you've been struck by the fear of decaying faucets and then rapidly uplifted by the benefits of boosted moods, let's get to work. You may have company visiting very soon. You might be dreaming of getting that vacation rental off the ground. You may be preparing yourself for an impending holiday season full of gatherings, gifts, and oh so much to do before then. Don't worry. The best time to start something new is right now. This book is going to bring you step-by-step into a new era for your home. Follow them closely to find the balance you seek. Each chapter of this book is structured for you to refer back whenever you need to refresh your strategy.

Relax, curl up, and let's get started on your journey to a new home.

Chapter 1: The Purpose of a Clean Home

You're here now with this book because you're ready for a change. You want a system of cleaning that you can not only live with, but enjoy. You may have tried your own system or that of another expert with poor results. You may have been skating by with the bare minimum because it's just not something that is taught like math or science. You may even be like I was: married to a routine until illness, an excess of work, or extracurricular activities took all of your free time. Whatever the reason, it is unique to you and your experience. The *importance* of a clean home will also depend on you and your situation. Take a moment now to ask yourself the question "Why is a clean home important to me?" After thinking for a few minutes, write down the top 3 reasons your mind rested on. You might think of more than 3, write those down, too. I'm willing to bet that there is a combination of personal and professional reasons on your list.

In the personal category, you may have written something related to being proud of your home. You're not alone in this. Your home reflects who you are and what makes you unique. You spend a large portion of your income on rent or a mortgage. You spend most of your time outside of work and on other activities in your home. It's where family gathers, pets spend their lives, and memories are made. It's no wonder a clean home is important to you! Your pride is simply a reflection of the many ways in which your home contributes to your life. You may not be in your "dream home" where the current inefficiencies and daily inconveniences are magically solved by new technology (or a better layout). However, listing pride as the reason is proof enough you have exactly what you need to love your home.

You may have also written down the desire for a presentable home whenever company comes calling. You find it important to be ready for guests on short notice. You may also just be tired of cycling through bare minimum everyday cleaning followed by a mad rush deep clean before family visits. Whatever the details, you're ready for the calm peacefulness that comes with a presentable home.

The importance of a clean home also has to do with your profession. A vacation rental lives or dies by reviews with one of the top categories being cleanliness. There are even separate categories in the review process dedicated to highlighting how clean or unclean the space. This isn't a surprise when you consider your own travels and what you rate as necessary for a pleasant hotel stay. You expect not only clean towels and fresh soap, but a fresh floor, pleasant scent, and no sign of previous occupants. Guests in your vacation rental expect the same.

Your professional reason may have more to do with a business you run out of your home. Clients and potential customers may visit on occasion. As they expect a clean environment when entering a commercial office space, they will want the same from your home office. Meeting and exceeding their expectations inspires trust and respect that translates into more work for your business. Even if your work doesn't involve client visits, the cleanliness of your environment affects the quality of what you produce. If you're unable to keep a baseline of clean in the space in which you operate, it becomes difficult to focus on your tasks. Eliminating the white noise from an untidy space will free up brain power to create quality work.

If you've read the last few paragraphs and failed to see where your home fits in, I invite you to consider the possibilities of a professional home. Your home may currently lack a professional purpose, but you will almost certainly define one at some point. For instance, if you are a member of a social club that rotates meeting locations and ends up at your home, you have created a professional purpose. When you volunteer for a community event, your home becomes the setting for other volunteers to gather and prep. If you're trying to recruit help for your service organization, your home turns into the informal meeting place where you win over new members.

When I sat down to make my own list of reasons why keeping a clean home is important to me, I found a mix of both personal and professional ones. I live in very close proximity to cousins, aunts, uncles, friends, and friendly neighbors. I also have a vacation rental out of a section of my home. When it came to managing the rental, I took the desires we all share when traveling and went from there. As I mentioned above, we all expect a clean environment when booking a hotel and rely on reviews to steer clear of unsavory accommodations. The same goes for private vacation rentals. Without the name brand to build trust and confidence, it's imperative to do everything possible to ensure a good review and high marks for cleanliness. After my first few bookings and high ratings, I found more requests hitting my inbox. The momentum kept up and so did my dedication to a clean space. I found that it didn't necessarily matter what color a bedspread was or if it matched the curtains. If people felt comfortable and clean in the space, they would say so and that would encourage potential customers to book.

Whether you use your property for personal or professional reasons, you'll find your "why" for keeping it clean. This book is here to help you put that "why" into action and start you on a journey to enjoying a clean home for years to come. Now that you're secure in your reasons and confident in your decision to make a change, let's tackle one of the biggest roadblocks to your clean future: anxiety.

If you're like me, you didn't receive a special education in cleaning and home maintenance. My grandmother, however, became my cleaning role model growing up. She was was classically trained to handle every aspect of house cleaning in addition to raising four children and working a full-time job.

As a kid, when gatherings and holidays were coming up, my parents and siblings would strive to get our house "Grandma Dot Clean." Even if I wasn't old enough to understand all my grandmother's tricks to a clean home, I knew the feeling of comfort and peace when walking through the door to a home like hers. It was a feeling that stuck.

Fast forward to college and summers working in the nation's capital. I was granted the immense privilege of staying in a family member's pied-a-terre during my summer internship. This responsibility became heavy, however, when I discovered my family would drop in without notice. After all, it was their place. But it switched something in me. I no longer had the cover of my upbringing or the excuse of a small dorm room to be messy. At that point, I only had the experience of cleaning houses for other people. I never established a routine for myself and my lifestyle. About to enter a new level of anxiety, I started small. I resolved to picking up after myself directly after using a space. After lounging on the couch watching TV, I'd make sure I folded the blanket and taken my water cup into the kitchen afterward. After making breakfast before work, I wiped every surface and cleaned each dish before I caught the bus.

That was how I made a turn away from cleaning anxiety and moved toward a zen-like attitude. We all have our own moments of anxiety around cleaning. You may have grown up in the cleanest house on the block, but found living on your own opened a sort of pandora's box of messiness. Whatever the case, it's important to start small. Picking up this book is the first small step. The next is a simple mind exercise.

To begin, find a comfy place to sit or lay down. You'll want to be able to relax each and every muscle. Next, take 10 slow breaths in and out. Breathe slowly and count each one to connect yourself with the rhythm. After your 10th breath, gather together the negative thoughts and associations with cleaning. Think of the failed attempts at establishing a routine. The seemingly endless task of keeping your home tidy. The embarrassment at paying guests or family members spotting dirt in your home. Think of the times you deep cleaned floors only to have a pet, child or partner create a mess soon after. Take all of those thoughts, memories, associations and acknowledge the negative feelings they inspire. Acknowledge those feelings and mentally send them on their way. Tell them they are no longer part of your present and have no place in your future.

Now, take 10 slow breaths in and out. Restore your body back to the relaxed state. After the 10th breath, imagine your home in its ideal state of cleanliness. The beds are made. The kitchen sink is empty. You can sit on your couch and see spotless floors into the next room. Immerse yourself in this vision by taking a mental tour of each room in your home, starting with the room you're in. Imagine what each room looks like perfectly clean. See the bedroom, bathroom, kitchen, living room, and even the closets. Don't miss out on the garage or storage closet, either. Take your time with this tour, absorb the positive feelings that swell within. Acknowledge those positive feelings that blossom during your mental tour. Invite them to stay and become part of your present and future.

Completing this mental exercise is just the beginning of the positive effects cleaning can have on your overall health. The simple act of envisioning a clean home helps put you in a mental state where you not only can function, but flourish in your cleaning routine. I mentioned a UCLA study in the introduction that found a relationship between clean homes and what owners say about their homes. The cleaner and more organized a home, the more positive things a homeowner had to say. The findings seem rational and matter-of-fact, but the simplicity of that connection is often overshadowed by the many ways cleaning can feel like an unwanted chore.

One way in which cleaning itself can help us step away from anxiety is through using cleaning as a mental break from our other work. In fact, a study from Florida State University found that mindfully washing dishes can calm the brain and decrease the stress you feel. The key word is "mindfully." Just as you tackled worrying thoughts and anxiety around cleaning, you can take on the act of cleaning itself with a bit of relaxed awareness.

The study focused on dishwashing, which for some people remains the most trying of household chores. However, the tactics of mindfulness can easily be applied to everything on your checklist. Carefully making your bed in the morning can help awaken your brain. It also gives you the first accomplishment for the day. With that achievement reached, you approach your work and other tasks with confidence. Rhythmically sweeping the floors or gliding the vacuum across them offers a repetitive physical motion that allows your brain to work on a mental problem. Whether stoking a creative flame or seeking an answer to a logic problem at work, the action gets blood flowing. At the end of the task, you may still be seeking the answer but will have found immediate accomplishment in the clean floors beneath your feet.

By now, you may either be feeling relaxed for the next steps or questioning how mental exercises translate into a clean home. Perhaps you're feeling a mix of both. The simple answer to both of those reactions is: I'll show you how. This book and every strategy within is more than just a random collection of factoids, anecdotes, and studies. It's the total guide to home cleaning that you'll refer to again and again. It's the encouraging friend who walks with you on a fulfilling journey. It's exactly what you need to start small and arrive at your final, clean destination.

Chapter 2: The Best Supplies For Every Surface

I have lived in 10 different rooms or apartments from the beginning of college to my home now. Each home or apartment was a different age with varying finishes and fixtures. Some were well cared for and required general cleaning. Others required deep cleaning and a trip to the hardware store to make them habitable. Each situation required its own set of cleaning supplies that worked best for the surfaces within. I developed this chapter using what I learned from my experience. There's a recommendation of products throughout starting with the most versatile, all-purpose cleaners. In the following chapter, I'll share my best recipes for homemade products. You should choose what works best for you and your home. This chapter is here to provide you with options.

All-Purpose Cleaners

These are first in the chapter because of their versatility. They can work in any room on most surfaces.

Method All-Purpose Cleaner® in various scents:

The choice in scents is plentiful and allows you to match the aroma to your preferences. According to the manufacturer, it is suited for most non-porous surfaces. When applied to a greasy kitchen countertop or toothpaste-laden bathroom sink, it performed admirably. This cleaner is not suited for grime build-up without the use of tools. It is possible to use too much at once, making the surface feel grimy from the cleaner and in need of a wipe down with a dry cloth. A key benefit is that it's non-toxic, which is naturally derived from biodegradable ingredients. With this benefit, it's an excellent choice for RV's, camping and homes with children and pets.

Trader Joe's Cedarwood and Sage All-Purpose Cleaner®:

Trader Joe's delivers on an affordable cleaning product without the unnatural looking neon color found in similarly priced cleaners. The scent is pleasant, but not overpowering. It does especially well on mirrors and windows. It performs its purpose without you worrying about putting too much on and leaving a new layer of cleaner grime. It's handy on non-porous surfaces such as sealed dining room tables, easily lifting dinner leftovers. It is also a plant based cleaner and biodegradable.

Mrs. Meyer's Multi-Surface Everyday Cleaner®:

The entire line of Mrs. Meyer's cleaners provides aromatherapy in addition to cleaning. The all-purpose cleaner comes in a variety of scents and the product performs well in most every application. Even if it can't remove all soap scum, it does leave it cleaner than before. One of the best parts of this cleaner is that you can purchase refills that are concentrated. This means less weight from excess water during shipping. The green trend continues with this product as it uses all biodegradable ingredients and sustainable sources wherever possible.

Purell Multi-Surface® Cleaner:

The name most associated with hand sanitizer applied the logic of sterilizing hands to the surfaces in your home. It is alcohol-based, requiring that it be used on non-porous surfaces. However, it doesn't need to be wiped down after use like other cleaners including Lysol® disinfecting wipes. It kills germs on contact, without needing you to wipe them away. This product is amazing in bathrooms, mud rooms, garages, and kitchens. Just be mindful of the surfaces!

Bathroom

Let's begin with the room that can be sanitized to hospital standards right after scrubbing but becomes a health hazard if not regularly cleaned. It's important to your family's health to keep a clean bathroom and even more important for vacation rental guests. Even if bathrooms are "clean," lurking rust stains, mildew spots, or soap buildup is a bad look for you and for your guests. The products used to clean should not only tackle grime and soap scum, but disinfect most if not all surfaces. There are a few tools you'll need to get the job done efficiently and quickly.

Solid Surfaces:

These surfaces are usually made of composite materials like Corian® or plastic veneer.

- Avoid abrasive materials if your surface was finished in a semi-gloss or gloss
- A non-greasy all-purpose cleaner will keep these surfaces clean
- If residue builds up, wipe down with a bleach cleaner like Soft Scrub®

MUST HAVE TOOL: Keep multiple rags in the same color closeby to wipe down surfaces after use. This will stave off deep cleans saving you time and effort down the road.

Acrylic:

Used for sinks, vanity tops, and showers, this surface is easy to clean and retains its new-in-box look for much longer than other materials like tile.

- This is one surface that needs disinfection
- After cleaning with a non-greasy all-purpose cleaner, wipe down with vinegar or bleach for disinfection
- Use a toothbrush to clean edges and caulk lines

MUST HAVE TOOL: Mr. Clean® Magic Eraser removes discolorations from soap scum with ease. Look for store brand equivalents to save a few dollars.

Stone and Granite:

Marble, quartz, granite, and limestone are the most common stone surface materials.
- Invest in a cleaner specific for stone and granite
- Always wipe down the surface after using a cleaner
- Marble and Granite: Take It For Granite® cleaner covers everything from floors to countertops
- Quartz: Use a window cleaner or all-purpose cleaner
- Limestone: Caldrea® Countertop Spray is perfect for non-porous surfaces like natural stone
- Use microfiber cloths to avoid scratches on all these surfaces

MUST HAVE TOOL: Razor blades make it easy to remove mineral stains and stuck on mess. Gently pass over the stains or mess several times until it wears down. Clean as usual.

Porcelain, Other Ceramics, and Cast Iron:

Old homes have cast iron sinks and tubs that may or may not need resealing. You can get either clean with the products below.
- Porcelain: an abrasive cleaner like Mrs. Meyers® Surface Scrub works wonders on set-in stains
- Toilets and bidets: a disinfecting cleaner like Method® Antibac Toilet gets rid of germs without the chemical smell using citric acid
- Tubs: A bleach cleaner like Soft Scrub® accomplishes a deep clean while an all-purpose cleaner is suitable for a regular cleaning

- Unsealed tubs and sinks: These get dirty, fast. Soft Scrub® or a vinegar baking soda mixture will take out stains until you can reseal

MUST HAVE TOOL: Use the following brushes for the best cleaning.
1. A toothbrush or similarly sized brush for small spaces
2. A handled stiff brush to cover more surface area.
3. A long-handled stiff brush to use leverage against a tough stain

EXTRA MUST HAVE TOOL: Keep a squeegee in your shower! This handy tool will keep soap from building up on tile, acrylic, and any other bath wall surface.

Faucets:

Nickel, chrome, brass, bronze, and stainless steel are the most common faucet finishes. They often come in either brushed or satin (shiny) variations. They can all use a wipe down with a cleaning rag after use to help prevent buildup and keep them sparkling between cleans. For grime and dirt removal, find an all-purpose cleaner that can disinfect without leaving residue behind. Try Purell Multi-Surface® Cleaner.

One common nuisance is the buildup of minerals where the faucet meets the sink or shower. It starts small and grows creeping out onto the surface of the sink or shower. Use an old toothbrush to scrub it during your regular cleaning. To get yourself to a baseline state of no buildup, use a metal cuticle tool found in nail grooming kits to gently scrape the buildup away.

Kitchen:

Depending on your lifestyle, the kitchen may be the most used room in your home. If you have one in your vacation rental, guests will use it for breakfasts and the occasional quick meal. It's perfectly normal for a kitchen to look lived in. Hardly anyone will strive to put away the dish drying rack between uses, but everyone can keep it empty after use.

Kitchen Surfaces

Stainless Steel:

Used for appliance faces, sinks and even countertops.
- The surface can be scratched, avoid abrasive tools and cleaners
- To get a streak-free clean on appliances and counters, use a stainless steel specific cleaner and don't be afraid to buff the surface with a soft cloth after cleaning
- Stainless sinks are susceptible to water marks if food, dishes, and water is left too long
- Make sure you wash dishes and rinse your sink soon after use to prevent marks

Porcelain-enameled:

Often found in the form of the popular farmhouse style sink.
- Avoid steel wool or scouring pads to protect the finish
- A plastic bristle brush is perfect for stains or stuck-on food
- For a deep-clean, use a gel cleaner that can sit and tackle stains like Mrs Meyers® Gel Cleaner or Soft Scrub®

Solid Surface:

Brand-name countertops, finishes on appliances, sinks, and vinyl laminate flooring.
- Avoid abrasive materials if your surface was finished in a semi-gloss or gloss
- A non-greasy all-purpose cleaner will keep these surfaces clean
- If residue builds up, wipe down with a bleach cleaner like Soft Scrub®

Tile:

May be used in countertops, backsplash, and flooring.
- Wipe down tile countertops after use to prevent grout stains
- A cleaner like Black Diamond® Marble and Tile will remove dirt and stains without leaving residue
- Backsplashes see a lot of food particles and should be wiped down after preparing and cooking food to prevent set-in stains

Stone and Granite:

Marble, quartz, granite, and limestone are the most common.
- Invest in a cleaner made for a stone surface
- Always wipe down the surface after using a cleaner
- Marble and Granite: Take It For Granite® cleaner covers everything from floors to countertops
- Quartz: Use a window cleaner or all-purpose cleaner
- Limestone: Caldrea® Countertop Spray is perfect for non-porous surfaces like natural stone
- Use microfiber cloths to provide extra softness to these surfaces

Wood:

Butcher blocks, counter tops, and even floors.
- Whether stand-alone or built into your countertop, butcher blocks need special care
- Howard® Butcher Block conditioner is food grade and should be applied regularly based on your use to keep the wood safe from food and other stains
- Wood floors in kitchens will already be sealed, but can be protected from accidental drops of heavy items (like mixing bowls or plates) with coordinating accent rugs

Favorite Kitchen Tools

Bona® mop kits:

Bona® makes simple non-smelly cleaners for your wood and tile surfaces making it the easiest system to use on all solid surface floors in your home. You can purchase multiple mopping pads to be able to clean all your floors in one go without leaving dirt behind. Throw them in the washer on a hot water cycle with regular laundry detergent. They're much more convenient than disposable ones and create less waste. You can also find generic versions of the mop, pads, and cleaner on janitor supply store websites. I recommend having a mop set (mop, a few pads, spray bottle of cleaner) on each level of your home or in each solid surface room.

Razor Blades:

Razor blades work exceptionally well on stuck burnt food on glass top ranges and even granite countertops. Be sure to go slowly and gently on surfaces that can scratch. Run the blade with light pressure back and forth over the stuck-on mess until it's broken up enough to remove with a soft cloth.

Cleaning Rags:

These will save your wallet on buying paper towels and plenty of trees. Make a set of at least 30 for your kitchen using old towels or t-shirts. If you can, choose one color to use in the kitchen and another color for any other room they're used in. This makes it easier to sort at laundry time and keep your bathroom rags from ending up in your kitchen.

Sink Grates:

Made of metal or silicone, sink grates sit at the bottom of your sink and keep dishes from directly touching the surface. This will not only keep your sink cleaner for longer, but protect any sealing on a new sink from wearing down sooner than it should.

Under Sink Storage:

Many kitchens now have intricate storage drawers, baskets, and more inside each cabinet. Even if you don't have sophisticated organization in other parts of your kitchen, invest in under sink storage. Specifically, a wire drawer made in a U-shape to avoid any plumbing and can slide out for a clear view of your supplies. This is a game changer for any kitchen. It's one of the most used rooms in the house, and thus, the most cleaned. You owe it to yourself to make finding supplies and tools easier.

Appliances

There were some appliances that fell under the surface categories above, but I want to dedicate a small section to everything that didn't fit there.

Ovens and Ranges:

If you have a gas range and find the cast iron grates difficult to clean, try a soak in hot water and dish detergent (like Dawn®) for 15 minutes before applying something like Goo Gone® Grill and Grate cleaner with a nylon or other plastic scouring pad. Ceramic grates can be soaked in the same solution and then scrubbed with a plastic-bristle brush to break up stains.

Refrigerators:

As soon as I learned you could take all the shelves and drawers out of a fridge, mine has never looked better – and for longer! Cleaning is simple with a plastic bristle brush and dish detergent. While the shelves are out, I warm up some wet rags in my microwave, put on some gloves and let the heat go to work cleaning off the worst food stains. After that, I take a disinfecting cleaner like Soft Scrub® or Purell® to wipe down the inside of the fridge. If you avoid cleaning your freezer because you think you have to let it thaw out completely, take advantage of the microwave and warm up wet rags. If ice buildup is especially thick, bring water to almost a boil on the stove and slowly pour into the bottom of the freezer where the build up occurred. This melts everything so you can quickly mop it up with a large towel.

Small Appliances:

My best trick to keeping these clean is storing them off the counter. I found myself constantly wiping down the mixer after preparing dinner, and I hadn't even used it in my prep! If that's not possible, designate a section of countertop that is only for food prep. Chopping, mixing and combining can all be done in one place while appliances live on other parts of the counter. Investing in a sturdy food cover will prevent spills while cooking.

Living Spaces:

Living rooms, home offices, and playrooms are some of the most common living spaces. They provide specific uses to make our time at home more enjoyable and productive.

Carpets and Rugs:

Carpet is a cozy choice for living spaces and easy to take care of with the right tools and tricks. For daily cleaning, invest in a good vacuum. It doesn't need to be a Dyson® either. I have found great success on low-pile and high-pile carpets with my Shark Navigator® Lift-Away® upright vacuum cleaner. It is economical and bagless (one less thing to keep on your shopping list). The canister design also makes it easy to clean with soap and water. It comes with a HEPA filter, in addition to, a sponge filter you can wash out every three months. A vacuum is only as good as the maintenance done to it, so no matter the brand follow the user's manual to ensure that each part is getting the recommended maintenance at the appropriate intervals. Invest in the accessories, too. You'll want a dust wand, an upholstery tool, and hose extensions for high ceilings.

What about hardwood or vinyl floors? I recommend a small canister vacuum like Eureka® Mighty Mite. It is a bag vacuum, but also one of the most effective vacuums in terms of suction and durability. I have had my vacuum for almost 10 years now and it still picks up pet hair, dust, and crumbs like a champ.

Rugs:

Rugs come in all price ranges thanks to improved manufacturing techniques and more affordable materials. Most store bought rugs will do fine with regular vacuuming and spot cleaning using Woolite® carpet cleaner. You can also take your rugs to be professionally cleaned every few years. For deep cleaning on wool rugs, professional cleaning is the only option because traditional methods (rented steam cleaners) leave too much water and can damage the wool. If you do have a stain on a wool rug, blot it (don't rub) with tepid water and a clean white towel.

Upholstered Furniture:

The fabric used on furniture is typically much more durable than the fabric used to make our clothing. It is also an item where you gain more durability and a longer lifespan as the price increases. Whether you have

IKEA® furniture or the latest from West Elm®, it's easy to keep them clean.

Most upholstery fabric will be blends of cotton, wool, and synthetic fibers. For those with leather, Mohawk® has a complete leather care and cleaning kit to tackle light surface scratches and discoloration.

For all other upholstery fabric, Woolite® makes a great upholstery cleaner to handle stains. To keep the fabric fresh and clear out any scents it absorbed, a spray of vinegar on the fabric will take on odors. Test a small area before spraying the rest of the upholstery. If you can remove cushion covers or any other fabric, wash on a delicate cycle using either Woolite® regular detergent or Woolite® Darks. These detergents will help keep the color in place so cushions that have been washed don't look a shade different from the rest of the upholstery.

Wooden or Veneer Furniture:

The product needed to care for wood furniture (and make it last for centuries) is so simple that most everyone overlooks it. All you need is a damp soft cloth that can be from an old towel or t-shirt. Wipe down each side of the wood and make sure to get in to each crevice to remove dust buildup. There are many wood cleaners marketed as must-haves but the reality is, wood is an easy clean. It doesn't need all of the fancy ingredients to make it shine. In fact, using cleaners like Pledge® and others actually builds up residue over time making your furniture look dull. Once a year (and only once a year), I will apply Old English® as a sort of extra barrier to dust and dirt. Other than that, it's a damp soft cloth for routine cleaning.

If your kitchen table is wood and you need to disinfect, use a solution of water and vinegar to spray it down. The ratio should be ¼ cup of vinegar to ¾ cup water. For painted wood, use a gentle all-purpose cleaner to remove spots and grime before wiping down with a damp soft cloth and letting it dry.

Lighting:

For fabric shades, use a dust wand vacuum attachment to take up the pet hair or dust that's collected. A lint roller (or traditional lint brush) can work well depending on the shape of the lamp shade.

For metal or glass sconces, remove them (if possible) and wipe them down with an all-purpose cleaner that doesn't leave streaks. If you can't remove them, grab your step stool and rise to them for cleaning.

Accessories:

I have to talk a little bit about plants because they are their own kind of cleaner. They keep indoor air from becoming polluted and bring in color to any room. Basic maintenance of plants is what I recommend to keep the area of the room they're in clean. Remove dead or dying leaves, branches and stems when they appear. This will prevent you having to vacuum them up later. Make sure the plants have a drainage plate or similar, if the species requires it. Keep them out of reach of pets to avoid them snacking on leaves and leaving a mess behind.

Anything not put away in a cabinet (printers, toys, figurines, vases, etc) requires some attention on a regular basis in order to avoid more intensive cleaning down the road. Invest in a microfiber duster and a few extra pads so you can dust these items at least once a week. Keeping the dust off of them now prevents it from building up and mixing with the moisture in the air to create a sort of dust icing. When it builds up to the dust icing point, you'll need a moist cloth and some time to wipe down each item.

Bedroom

Bed:

Your bed will most likely take up the biggest surface area, which means there's a lot of floor underneath that doesn't get attention when you vacuum. If you have the additional hose extensions for your vacuum, you should be able to reach underneath your bed. If your bed is particularly low or hard to reach, you may want to consider an area rug to put underneath. This will allow dirt, hair, and dust to get caught on the outer edges of the carpet before they reach under the bed.

Bedside Tables:

I advocate for bedside tables with drawers to keep necessary items close at hand and out of sight for a cleaner look. However, glasses, phones, and jewelry can somehow end up scattered on top. If that's the case with you, keep all other clutter off these surfaces and make space for these items. A small decorative jewelry tray keeps rings and other loose items safe. I also recommend a Diamond Dazzle® stick to dust off jewelry.

Room for your phone becomes designated with a wireless charging pad. The case you brought your glasses home with becomes a safe place for spectacles. In order to keep these items clean and organized, stock cleaning pads for your phone and microfiber cloth for glasses. Cleaning these often-used items daily will keep germs away and your vision clear.

Curtains, Blinds, and Shutters:

You more than likely have window coverings in every room of your house, but they're especially necessary in bedrooms. Keep them in top shape, whether in the bedroom or living room.

Fabric Curtains:

For any visible dust, use the dust wand attachment on your vacuum while holding the curtain to gently vacuum up dust. Once a year, you can air out the curtains in the sun or put them in the dryer for a 20 minute cycle. If they are washable, feel free to also wash them before airing out.

Blinds and Shutters:

For deep cleaning, I recommend a warm bowl of water and vinegar applied gently with soft cloths. It is tedious, but if you keep up with regular dusting, you'll be able to go longer between these deep cleans. Using a microfiber duster, you can safely swipe between each blind without damage. You'll be able to pick up a lot with the microfiber as you perform this task.

Bedding:

As dirt collects on us and our pets, it's important to wash your sheets once a week. Dirt and dust buildup on sheets can irritate skin and aggravate allergies. Duvet covers should also be washed weekly while duvet inserts can be washed once a year. If possible, change your shower routine to the evenings to keep your sheets fresh all week long.

Air:

If you're getting the recommended 8 hours of sleep, that's ⅓ of your day spent in your bedroom. Clean air is especially important in this room where so much time is spent. Add houseplants to help clean the air and invest in a quiet air purifier to really keep the air fresh

Small Spaces:

Entryways, hallways, mudrooms, and other small spaces also need attention. Wherever possible, I like to use cleaners and tools across multiple rooms. In that spirit, you'll find the recommendations for surfaces you have in these spaces by referring back to other rooms in the chapter. However, there are some unique tips and tools for small spaces.

Machine washable rugs in high-traffic areas like entryways, hallways, and mudrooms are a must to keep stains away (and your mind at ease). Machine washable rugs also tend to be a bit more affordable than other kinds, allowing you to pick up a few extra rugs to rotate and keep your floors covered at all times. For every rug in a high-traffic area, I recommend having one backup.

Upright canister vacuums work wonders in these spaces. Because of their high-traffic nature, dirt from the outside builds up quicker than elsewhere in the house. By keeping one of these vacuums in the nearest coat closet, you can quickly clean up any dirt.

There are new cleaning products hitting shelves and social media advertisements everyday. When researching and trying out new products, I often wished there was someone who could just tell me what to use in each scenario. This chapter is my own version of that much sought-after advice and the rest of the book builds on it. By the time you finish this book, you'll no longer wonder what to use and where.

If you went out and bought everything in this chapter today you'd likely blow your cleaning budget for the entire year. To avoid that, take in these new products slowly. You may already have a great vacuum, but maybe it needs some TLC. Skip the new vacuum and go right for the set of cleaners that will make your bathroom sparkle. For any old products, make sure you dispose of them properly in a local hazardous waste recycling center.

Chapter 3: DIY Cleaning Mixes

Your cleaning supplies storage may look like a disaster right now. It may be one of the biggest reasons you committed to changing how you clean. It's so easy to pick up a spray bottle from the alluring display at the end of the store aisle. You might have tried a product based on a recommendation from a friend but found it useless. These products stack up under sinks and in closets. I committed to using up all the products I had in my home. When that wasn't possible, I properly disposed of any leftover items (following my local hazardous waste disposal guidelines).

I urge you to do the same and work your way through the stacks of ineffective cleaners, replacing each one with recipes found in this chapter and the store-bought items from the previous chapter. Taken together, the list of products provides choice for every household cleaning need. There are mothers who worry about using bleach in the same bathtub they bathe their children. There are new apartment dwellers who are stuck with the unfortunate task of deep cleaning a bathroom that was previously neglected. Each phase of our life will require different products. The cleaning recipes in this chapter fit a multitude of applications. They also are easy on your budget and use ingredients you can find in grocery stores.

Cleaning Ingredients:

The recipes in this chapter all take ingredients from this list. Feel free to use it as a shopping list and stock up.

- Lemon juice
- Distilled white vinegar
- Baking soda
- Borax
- Bleach
- Isopropyl alcohol
- Natural dish soap
- Glycerin
- Olive oil

Cleaning Recipes

Bathroom

Bathrooms are one of the most important rooms to sanitize. The recipes I've found keep that in mind and offer non-chemical options to disinfect surfaces. I've also included a few that will get you to a basic level of clean you can easily maintain.

The-Stains-Are-Not-Mine Grout Cleaning Recipe:

- 1tbsp of baking soda
- ½ tbsp bleach

This recipe is great for tile in bathrooms and kitchens. Because it uses bleach, I mix the ingredients together in the amounts listed creating a small amount of paste. Drip that or scoop with your scrub brush onto the grout. Most stains will scrub out immediately, but if needed, let the mix sit for 10 minutes before trying to scrub. I highly recommend this method when moving into a new home or apartment. You can also do it as preparation for re-sealing your grout, which should be done periodically to prevent deep set stains and prolong the life of the grout.

Everyday Cleaning Tile and Grout Recipe:
- 2 cups water
- 2 cups vinegar
- 1tbsp natural dish soap

Mix the water and vinegar together in a spray bottle before adding the dish soap.

This recipe is perfect for weekly tile and grout cleaning in your bathroom. It also works well cleaning the backsplash in your kitchen. It will remove soap scum in your bathroom while tackling food grease buildup in your kitchen.

Tip: If you have unglazed tiles that are more textured, you'll need a recipe that can tackle the dirt inside all the nooks and crannies. Mix half a cup of baking soda into a bucket of warm water (about a gallon) and wipe down with a soft cloth letting the baking soda do the scrubbing.

Water Scale Rescue:
- ¼ cup vinegar
- ¾ cup hot water (not boiling)
- 1 tbsp natural dish soap

Mix all ingredients together in spray bottle. Spray the fixture or area and let soak for 5 minutes before rinsing. Wash shower liners with vinegar and hot water in your washing machine to get the same effect

Hard-To-Reach Cleaner:

- 1 cup lemon juice

Dip a toothbrush into lemon juice to clean grime and water marks inside the metal tracks of shower doors, on shower curtain rods, and other shower door hardware.

Mineral Deposit Remover:

- Varying amounts of vinegar

Whether on your faucets or showerhead, a soak in straight vinegar will loosen deposits and allow you to scrub them away with a toothbrush or straight pin.

Toilet Cleaner:

- 1/2 cup of white vinegar

Utilize the disinfectant properties of white vinegar for everyday toilet cleaning. If cleaning up a ring where the water meets the bowl, let a half cup of vinegar sit for a few hours before scrubbing.

Kitchen

Preparing raw meat and produce both require a sanitized environment to protect your health. These recipes keep that in mind with simple ingredients and easy applications. I also included a few recipes that took me years to find, including one to clean your oven. My favorite is the all-purpose disinfecting cleaner that can be made with any desired scent using essential oils.

All-Purpose Disinfecting Cleaner:

- ½ cup water
- ½ cup white vinegar
- 2 tbsp fresh lemon juice (you can substitute 12-24 drops of a preferred essential oil for the lemon juice)

This cleaner is perfect for the kitchen (and bathroom) because it not only cuts grease, but can disinfect. This is essential in any kitchen that is prepping raw food.

Note: Vinegar will dull the shine of granite and other stone countertops. Mix a recipe of half water and half isopropyl alcohol to disinfect and clean granite while protecting the surface.

Ultimate Non-Abrasive Disinfecting Oven Cleaner:

- 2 cups baking soda
- ½ cup borax

Store dry mix in a glass container. Sprinkle onto oven mess and then spray area with water from a spray bottle. Scrub with a plastic bristle brush.

Marble Counter Cleaner:

- ⅓ cup liquid fabric softener
- ⅔ cup water.

Mix ingredients together in a spray bottle and apply to marble surface, wipe clean with a cloth, and then polish with a soft cloth.

Living Areas

Living areas include everything from dining rooms to bedrooms and even the laundry room. These recipes help to tackle dirt on windows, floors, and even inside washing machines.

Spot-Free Window Cleaner:
- 2 cups water
- ¼ cup vinegar.

Mix ingredients in a spray bottle. Spray windows and wipe down with a reusable cloth.

Tip: If you've been cleaning your windows with store-bought cleaners, they more than likely contain ingredients that build up into a wax film on your windows. It may take several cleanings, and cloths to get this layer of wax off and your windows sparkling.

Non-Wood Floor Cleaner:
- ¼ cup natural liquid soap
- ½ cup vinegar
- 2 gallons of hot water

Combine all ingredients. If using a traditional mop, mix ingredients in a bucket. If using a dry mop, combine into spray bottles. This recipe is perfect for vinyl, linoleum, and even tile.

Wood Floor Cleaner:
- ¼ cup natural liquid soap
- ½ cup glycerin
- 2 gallons of hot water.

Combine all ingredients. If using a traditional mop, mix ingredients in a bucket. If using a dry mop, combine into spray bottles.

Tip: Try a natural liquid soap with essential oils in it for an even better smell and some aromatherapy while cleaning.

Deep Carpet Cleaner:

- ⅛ cup natural liquid soap
- 2 gallons of water
- Add ½ tsp of borax to tackle especially dirty carpets.

This formula is meant for use in professional or home carpet cleaners. It gives you an effective cleaner with less chemicals than standard concentrates. You can also add essential oils for a fresh scent.

Tip: Rent a carpet cleaner from a local retailer and use this formula to save $15-20 on the retailer's cleaning concentrate.

Wood Furniture Polish:

- 2 cups olive oil
- 1 cup lemon juice.

Mix ingredients in a bowl. Apply with a soft cloth to lessen scratches before buffing with a different soft cloth.

Washing Machine Sanitizer:

- 1 and 1/4 cup vinegar
- 1 quick clean cycle with hot water.

Pour 1 cup vinegar directly into washer drum and ¼ cup vinegar into soap dispenser. Wash on a quick wash cycle (about 30 minutes) with hot water.

After reading this chapter, you'll be amazed at what can be tackled with less than 10 ingredients. I hand selected each recipe based on its own impact in my home and because I believe in owning cleaners with less chemicals. In some cases, heavy-duty cleaners like bleach are needed to get a room back to a clean state. In those cases, make sure the area is well-ventilated and look into a mask that will help filter any fumes or smells from the cleaner. Once an area is back to basic cleanliness, use these recipes to keep them sparkling.

Chapter 4: Decluttering Steps You Can't Skip

Gathering the right cleaners, recipes, and tools is the beginning of a great cleaning experience. The next step is to declutter each area in preparation for cleaning. Even the most dedicated person will have some clutter to move around in each room before beginning their cleaning regimen. To avoid getting caught up in the mess and losing precious time picking things up, make decluttering part of your routine. Give yourself a set amount of time when cleaning each room to take care of things left behind from previous use. Each room has a list of tips to follow and when completed together, take less than 10 minutes. It's the perfect warmup before cleaning begins.

Bathroom

Designate a Cleaning Basket: Your bathroom may have multiple drawers and cabinets making it easy to store frequently used items out of sight. You may also keep a certain number of products and tools on your counter or sink for easy access. No matter the setup, the quickest way to declutter a bathroom is by using a plastic basket. Placing all the products and tools into the basket keeps them in one place while cleaning. When finished, you can take each item out individually, giving you a moment to notice if a bottle is empty or if an item belongs in another room. This same method also applies for cleaning your bath or shower.

Keep a Hamper in Sight: A hamper in the bathroom may already be part of your home organization. If not, make it happen. Quickly decluttering clothes in your bathroom depends on ease of storage. A nearby hamper organizes your clothes ready to be washed and allows you to start cleaning faster.

Make Room for Jewelry and Watches: It's easy to have jewelry and watches pile up in a bathroom. They begin to stack up on countertops, the backs of toilets, and on shelves. Designate one spot to keep jewelry worn frequently, preferably in a jewelry box.

Take Out the Trash: Remove the liner from your bathroom trashcan and pick up loose trash on counters, floors, and shelves. After taking out the trash, you avoid having to stop the cleaning process to pick up peeled product labels, beauty store receipts, and product packaging.

Kitchen

It's easy for a kitchen to look like it's been neglected for a week after just one meal. If you gave yourself the night off and wake up in the morning needing to get it back in shape, don't worry. Follow these steps and you'll have a clean kitchen in no time.

Stack the Dishes: The only time my sink, dishwasher, and dish rack are empty of dishes is for an hour after the Thanksgiving meal. With so many cooks in the kitchen preparing a feast fit for the holiday, you get an equal amount of cleaners. Every dish is washed, dried, and put away before the holiday football game reaches halftime. But this only happens once a year. On days that are not Thanksgiving, it's important to not be overwhelmed by dishes standing between you and cleaning your kitchen. If your sink is nearly empty, grab all the dirty dishes around the kitchen and stack them in the sink. If your sink is full, empty the dishwasher or dish rack and set a time for 5 minutes to wash (or load as many dishes as you can). This clears your counters and lets you tackle the full task of emptying the sink at the end of your cleaning regimen. With the rest of the kitchen clean, you can't help but tackle the dishes and finish off the space.

Move from Left to Right: Most kitchen counters have temporary clutter like cereal boxes or other food. They also have more permanent clutter including utensil holders and small appliances. To truly tackle every spot of counter space, start on the farthest left section of counter. Move all clutter to a section of counter on the right. Clean the bare counter and then replace the appliances and other items. Start on the far left and use the left to right motion to give you momentum until the space is clean. Avoid moving countertop clutter to a kitchen table or to a designated spot on the other side of the kitchen, as it is more time consuming.

Get Rid of Papers: Printed recipes, mail, and magazines can stack up quickly in a kitchen. Before you can start cleaning, you need to gather all the paper in the kitchen in one spot to sort later. Find a basket or small bin and go around the space to find all the paper. If you find items that belong in different rooms, put them together in their own separate basket to be sorted later. These baskets are not a new version of a junk drawer. Instead, they offer a quick way to corral items before sorting them.

Pick Up Pet Bowls: Food and water bowls for pets are often found in the kitchen. Before you begin cleaning, take up the bowls and put them in the sink. If you're taking time to clean the kitchen, it's also a great opportunity to clean out the food and water bowls for your pets.

Living Room

Your living room can end up being the catchall for everything that doesn't belong. This includes coats that should be on the coat rack or in the mud room. A pile of clean laundry that got stuck on the way from the dryer to your dresser drawers. Empty boxes from mail delivery. Books, bags, and even shoes that ended up tucked into corners. This may be the most daunting room to clean because of the immense buildup of clutter. Strip that title away with these simple tips (and a mindful touch).

Bring-Your-Own Trash Can: Save yourself time and trouble by bringing in a lined wastebasket before you even begin cleaning. It is crucial to keep with you while carrying out the following tips.

Mail, Magazines, Memorabilia: Remember the basket you used for decluttering paper in the kitchen? It should be empty now and ready to collect postcards, open letters, and random paper building up in the living room. Go through the room picking up each piece of paper and immediately tossing useless ones in the wastebasket. If you're not sure if a paper or magazine is worth keeping, put it in the basket. The goal of this decluttering method is to do it quickly. Save the thoroughness for when you're emptying the basket of paper.

Choose a Back (Chair or Couch): You've already spent time bringing in a trash can and a basket to collect clutter. Don't waste anymore time by bringing in a clothes hamper, too. Take any coats, clothes, or blankets and lay them in a pile on a chair or section of the couch. Move them during cleaning when you need to reach the section they're on before sorting them at the end.

Toys and More Toys: Whether you have human children, animal children, or a combination of both, toys are a natural accessory to the space. In the living room, they can take up large sections of floor making it impossible to carry on with your cleaning. Each living room should have a toy basket to not only teach children the necessary task of tidying up, but to easily collect toys before cleaning.

Bedroom

The items you keep in your bedroom typically have a home. Jewelry boxes keep precious pieces safe. Dressers store non-hanging clothes. A vanity table collects the perfumes and beauty products used daily. It's more than easy, however, for these items to end up all over the room.

The best and most simple way to declutter a bedroom is by first ensuring each bedroom item has a home. Then, when preparing to clean, set a time for 10 minutes to put as many things back in their homes as possible. For items that don't belong in the bedroom, use the same decluttering basket from the kitchen and living room to store the items in one place. After cleaning, take them to their designated spots in the rest of your home.

Laundry Room

It's so easy to take even the most organized laundry room and turn it into a disaster over the course of normal use. Before getting down to cleaning spilled soap and runaway lint, take a moment to pick up clutter.

Clothes: Keep an extra hamper in your laundry room, preferably one that folds flat. Use it to gather together the random assortment of line dried clothes, loose socks, and other linen. Empty it after cleaning to get each item back to its home.

Cleaning Products: While you may not keep all the cleaning products for your home in the laundry room, the ones that do live there are probably in bins or loose on shelves. You may even store them in baskets that are then placed on those same shelves. No matter the case, when it's time to deep clean and wipe down their storage, get them on the floor. Starting with the highest shelf or basket, remove all products and place them on the floor. Moving from top to bottom keeps dust and dirt from falling off a higher shelf to a lower one you just cleaned.

Home Office

Your home office may be the epicenter of productivity and still look like the aftermath of an earthquake. It's important to keep this area clean, especially if you work from home. Keeping dirt and dust down in this room helps keep the air healthy while you're putting in hours for work.

The quickest way to declutter in preparation for cleaning is with designated baskets. One for papers, one for books and one for items that belong elsewhere. Use the baskets from the kitchen and living room to cut down on extra baskets laying around that force you to empty them after each use. Collect papers from all over the room in one basket. Take books that need reshelving or magazines that need categorizing and put them in another basket. If you have items that belong in a different room like an item of clothing, shoes, blanket or other, gather them in one basket. At the end of cleaning, take this basket around the house until each item has found its home again.

Decluttering a space before cleaning is most often an exercise in triage. You're doing what you can with the time you have to achieve the best possible result. When you start out on the journey to find a regular cleaning schedule for your home, it will feel overwhelming. That's okay. You are building a routine to last you a lifetime and that doesn't happen overnight. The decluttering tips in this chapter are meant to get you over one of the biggest hurdles on your way to a lifetime cleaning routine: the piles of clutter that exist now. Your cleaning routine may one day skip most if not all of these decluttering tips. You might find yourself doing dishes as you use them preventing a pile-up in the sink. You might begin sorting mail at the mailbox keeping junk out and important items filed away immediately. You will find the balance that works for you and your lifestyle. In the meantime, this chapter is everything you need to get started today. Remember that starting small means you're already on your way to big things.

Chapter 5: Kitchen

A kitchen often serves as the center of a home. Even small kitchens draw family and friends during meal preparation and clean up. Even when you're not entertaining, the space serves you and your family throughout the day. Despite the heavy use, it's one of the easiest rooms in your home to keep clean. Unlike other rooms in your home, the messes created in the kitchen are easily tackled while working on other important tasks. When cooking most everyday meals, there is inevitably downtime during the process. While waiting for water to boil for pasta, you can stir the pasta sauce before unloading or loading the dishwasher. When I've finally assembled vegetables for roasting, hit the button to start the timer and finish not only meal prep cleanup but the daily wipedown of all the counters.

Thanks to the ease of multitasking in the kitchen, this chapter is especially motivating and provides a number of ways to make best use of your time. In this chapter and the ones after, I've organized the usual cleaning tasks associated with each space into categories based on time and surface. In doing so, you'll be able to determine what you can do in the time you have. Each set of times, tasks, and surfaces gets your space ready for guests.

It's easy to find yourself in a situation where even with a whole day's notice, there's only a short amount of time available to clean. The rest of your schedule demands attention leaving you stressed about visiting guests. In this section, I break down cleaning tasks in your kitchen by the time it takes to do them. Even if you only have 10 minutes to spare, you can make an impact in your space. Pick and choose each cleaning task based not only on the time you have available, but your immediate needs. If your sink is empty, but your counters cluttered, then tackle the clutter. There are multiple tasks in each category allowing you to mix different tasks together to equal the amount of time you have. If you have half an hour of time, you can complete both a 10 minute cleaning task *and* a 20 minute cleaning task.

10 Minute Clean

Clear counters: Putting food away, clearing trash, and moving dishes to the sink can give you a clear line of sight around the kitchen before you even pick up a cleaning cloth. If you do have time leftover, you can wipe down the counters.

Wipe down appliances: Starting with the larger appliances like ranges, dishwashers, and refrigerators, wipe down appliance fronts with a soft cloth and your favorite cleaner. If you have more time, move on to smaller appliances like blenders, toasters, and microwaves.

20 Minute Clean

Unload and load the dishwasher and/or dishrack: Clearing out your sink gives an instant boost to the look of your kitchen. It not only declutters dishes, but cleans them.

Bonus time: Keep your favorite sink cleaner close at hand so you can clean the sink.

Sweep and mop floors: A broom is easier to set up than a vacuum, so grab it out of the closet and start sweeping. When finished, tackle any spots on the floor before using a dry mop with your favorite cleaner to mop the area.

30 Minute Clean

Clear the counters: With half an hour, you can tackle everything on your counter. Move dishes to the sink and trash to the receptacle. Working clockwise, wipe down counters around the kitchen. Empty the countertop dish rack, if you have one. Take any clutter found and put it away where it belongs, even if it lives in a different room.

Clean inside appliances: Tackle the crumbs and food residue buildup in all your small appliances. Clean out your toaster oven, microwave, bread toaster, coffee maker, and anything else that collects crumbs. If you have more time, wipe down any other small appliance that could use an exterior clean. Blenders, hand mixers, and any other countertop appliances can pick up food residue during meal prep or clean up.

Building a Cleaning Schedule

This section breaks down even more cleaning tasks, including deep cleaning, to provide you the pieces you need to put together a cleaning schedule. Part of a successful cleaning schedule and the trick I use to keep my own home clean involves doing a little bit each day. In this kitchen chapter, as well as the chapters on other rooms, I've defined cleaning times for the most common tasks. Using that knowledge, you can build your weekly and even monthly cleaning schedule. Some tasks, like cleaning out the fridge, should be done once a month or every other week. Other tasks, like vacuuming floors, should be done more frequently. Start with the time you're allowing for cleaning your home each day, whether it's an hour or 30 minutes, and build these tasks in with the ones for other rooms. This chapter and the next few are like a buffet of options meant to help you find what works best for your home.

This section will also give you the best methods for cleaning everything from garbage cans to stovetops. Each method was developed to save time and strain, making cleaning a breeze.

Appliances

Countertop appliances (30 minutes): Tackle the crumbs and food residue buildup in all your small appliances. Clean out your toaster oven, microwave, bread toaster, coffee maker, and anything else that collects crumbs. Wipe down the exterior. Blenders, hand mixers, and any other countertop appliances can pick up food residue during meal prep or clean up. Wipe their exteriors and remove all grease and food spots.

Refrigerator (1 hour): Start by clearing out old or expired food. Empty food storage containers and stack them next to the sink. Once the fridge contents have been pared down, start from the top of the fridge and work your way down removing each shelf to wash it in the sink. Use soap and water. As you work your way down from the top of the fridge, use a cloth wet with hot water to tackle food stains. Then take your favorite disinfecting cleaner and clean each area of the fridge. Next, turn your focus to the exterior. If the exterior is cluttered with papers and magnets, remove them all. Go through and get rid of any that are out of date or no longer useful. While the magnets are off, find your favorite all-purpose cleaner and wipe down the exterior, including the handles and the gaskets. The gaskets are the rubber material used to frame the door and ensure an airtight seal when the fridge and freezer sections are closed.

Tip: refrigerator handles should be cleaned weekly to cut down on germs, while a deeper cleaning can be done once a month.

Stove (2-12 hours): You can follow the directions on a store bought oven cleaner to tackle the mess from overflowing dishes. You can also use the Ultimate Non-Abrasive Disinfecting Oven Cleaner from chapter 3 to take on any messes in your oven and see it shine again. If you're deep cleaning your oven on a regular basis, say once a month, it's good to let the oven cleaner recipe sit overnight on the food buildup. The next day you can clean it up while also wiping down the oven walls. To keep food from building up in your oven between deep cleanings, set a timer for 30 minutes after a spill to allow the oven to cool. Once the temperature of the oven walls is lowered enough that you can wipe the surface safely, wet a cloth and clean up the mess. Tackling the biggest part of a food spill in an oven will keep spills from heating and smoking during future cooking cycles.

Dishwasher (1 hour): The actual time cleaning the dishwasher is probably 10 minutes, but involves running the dishwasher for a cycle in the middle. Start out by checking the trap for any food pieces that did not dissolve during wash cycles. Fill the detergent reservoir with white vinegar and run it through a cycle, but leave out the drying part at the end to save a little energy. When completed, sprinkle borax in the bottom and with a soft brush or cloth, wipe down the walls of the dishwasher.

Behind appliances (30 minutes): Take care of the spaces behind appliances to keep odors from food messes and air allergens down. For the oven, carefully slide away from the wall. If you're not sure of the floor's scratch resistance, use cut up rags to slide under the front feet of the oven. Use a second person to push up on the oven to be able to slide the rags under the feet. If you have a gas stove, be mindful of the connection and don't overextend it by moving your range out too far. Once you have moved the stove a safe distance back from the wall, use a vacuum with a scrap of pantyhose covering the end to pick up large items. Remove the scrap and then vacuum the rest. Using a dry mop, mop the area behind the stove. If you are able to move the stove completely out, you'll be able to get more of the floor. This method is for open space you're able to create behind the appliance for cleaning.

For your fridge, carefully slide it away from the wall. Avoid jostling or tipping to prevent the coolant inside from moving around too much and ending up in the wrong components. You should be able to remove it completely from the wall accessing the full square footage it occupies when in place. If not, defer to the oven instructions for careful cleaning of the area you can access. For cleaning the full area, use a vacuum or broom to collect any dust or dirt. Use your favorite floor cleaner to wipe down the floor. Use your favorite duster to dust the walls surrounding the fridge.

Floors and Windows

Vacuum or Sweep (15 minutes): Depending on your equipment and floor size, it may be faster to use a broom and sweep. Vacuums can be faster, depending on how easily accessible it is. Either way, this task takes about 15 minutes or less.

Dry mop (15 minutes): Dry mopping is the fastest way to get the deep set dirt off the floor. Use a Bona® or off-brand alternative mop system that includes washable pads and a broom-length handle. It doesn't take a lot of storage and can be accessed quickly. Use it with your favorite floor cleaner in a spray bottle avoiding the lengthy drying times of wet mopping.

Windows (10 minutes): Take your favorite window cleaner, homemade or store bought, and lightly spray all your windows. Let them set as you work your way through the panes of all your kitchen windows. Take a soft cloth and wipe in a circular motion.

Deep Cleaning

Trash receptacle (15 minutes): You may have a simple plastic can that sits under the sink or a plastic liner inside of a can with a lid. If you have more than just the standalone plastic can, add about 5 more minutes to the deep cleaning time. Start by removing any leftover garbage pieces from the bin. Then, using your favorite disinfectant spray, spritz the inside of the bin and let sit. Turn on the hot water in your kitchen sink and prop up the bin on one side of the sink. Wash the inside with your cleaning brush (not the one used on dishes) and dish soap. To clean the outside, spritz with your favorite disinfectant cleaner and wipe down with a soft cloth to dry. Once dry, sprinkle some baking soda in the bottom of the bin to help soak up odors and fight moisture.

Sink faucet (10 minutes): This area of your kitchen can become especially grimy and water-stained after heavy use. To restore the shine, take your favorite cleaner with degreasing power and cover the faucet. Use one that is thick and coats the surface. Wait two minutes and start wiping the faucet with a soft cloth. Work slowly ensuring each spot has been reached. If there is any cleaning residue leftover, take a clean damp cloth and wipe down the faucet. Polish with a clean dry cloth to remove any further moisture.

Cabinet faces (1-4 hours): The time it takes for this task is dependent on how many cabinets are in your kitchen. In a large kitchen with both upper and lower cabinets throughout, 4 hours will be a correct estimation of time. With a stack of soft cloths and a good wood cabinet polishing solution (like Wood Magic Furniture Cleaner and Polish®), work your way clockwise on the upper cabinets. Open doors and drawers to reach areas hidden when doors are closed. Move on to the lower cabinets working in the same clockwise direction. Cleaning and polishing will not only remove grease and food residue, but leave a protective barrier and sheen behind.

Butcher blocks (15 minutes): Invest in a good wax-and-oil product and using a soft cloth, apply to your butcher block. Wait 20 minutes and wipe off excess. You should perform this each time the wind starts to dry out.

Countertops (1 hour): You may be able to complete this in less than an hour depending on the surface area of your counters, but an hour is typical for this multi-step deep clean. After clearing the counter of any items, begin by dispensing a gentle dish soap on the counter. Wet a soft cloth in warm water and begin cleaning the counter in a circular motion. Use a razor (stone and granite counters) or a plastic tool (composite or other hard surface counters) to remove any stuck on food. Rinse your soft cloth in warm water to begin wiping away the soap mess. After your counter is free of soap and excess water, wipe down with a dry cloth. If you have stone counters, including granite, take your favorite stone-safe disinfectant and spray onto counters. Wipe with a clean cloth. Using your favorite polish safe for your counter surface, apply to counters with a soft cloth for an even better sheen.

These deep cleaning techniques are done on a rotating basis in my home. Rather than adhering to a schedule tied to time, I employ them on the basis of use. If I have a weekend of hosting guests with all the meals to go with, I'll spend time starting Monday through the rest of the week taking on one task at a time. You don't want to spend the following weekend cleaning up from the previous, so take chunks of time during your week to complete important deep cleaning tasks.

Many people think the only way you can have a clean and presentable kitchen is by putting in multiple hours deep cleaning every surface. Thankfully, the truth is a lot more simple. By breaking up kitchen tasks into routine cleaning and deep cleaning, you can have a guest-ready kitchen at a moment's notice. Even when life gets in the way of your regular routine, there are simple ways to tidy up quickly. Use the kitchen advantage of multitasking to stay motivated. The results are rewarding for both you and your guests.

Chapter 6: Living Areas

The number of uses for a living space, including the traditionally titled living room, is expansive. This space can be solely dedicated to proper seating to support socializing when guests are over. It can also shift shape depending on the needs of the day. Seating for a large group can give way to workspace for a large hands-on project. Keeping the space clean and ready for your next project or visit from houseguests requires a few thoughtful strategies. The pressure points in a living area will differ from every other room in the home. This chapter will identify those points and provide effective solutions to taking the pressure off them.

Three pressure points of a living room:

Dust: Dust is composed of many ingredients from your environment. It is the collection of your hair, skin cells, fur from pets, dirt, and so much more. The amount of dust that collects will depend on your environment. A home with pets will have more dust building up faster than homes without pets. A home with 6 people living in it will have more dust than a home with just one person.

To get ahead of the dust in your home, there are 2 things you can do right now. The first is to ensure all your air filters are changed on a regular basis. The general rule is that the thicker the filter, the longer it can go without changing. Some filters need to be changed monthly while others last up to 6 months. Determine the rating on your filters and schedule their replacement accordingly. No matter what the filter manufacturer recommends, you'll need to also assess your home in deciding when to replace filters. With multiple pets and people, your air filter may need to be changed out more often.

The second thing applies to households with pets. If you have cats and dogs, it's important to brush them on a regular basis. A weekly brushing with a Furminator® or similar brush will remove excess fur not only from the top coat, but the layer beneath. If it's difficult to keep your pet still for a long period of time to brush them, keep a small brush close at hand and perform the task in short increments throughout the week.

In terms of dusting tools, invest in a microfiber duster that not only attracts dust as it moves over surfaces, but can be washed after use. This saves you money over time by foregoing frequent purchases of disposable cloths. It also means you don't run out of cloths requiring you to go to the store just to get your cleaning finished. If you have a ceiling fan in your living area, an extendable tool with a special attachment is worth purchasing. This tool is made to glide over each fan blade capturing dust and making the job quick. I say it's worth investing in because of the time saved over a traditional method of bringing out a step-ladder and wiping each blade down by hand.

For objects on surfaces, dust them before dusting surfaces. Just as you want to dust your home from top to bottom (if you have multiple levels), you want to dust your objects and surfaces in the same way. This will keep dust falling to each successive level rather than stirring it up to sit on a surface you already dusted.

Clutter: One of the best ways you can stay on top of clutter is by designating a home for everything in it. There will be activities that always take place in the living area, like board games and movie watching. Find storage solutions for the objects that support those activities. For activities that are done in multiple parts of the home, like laundry folding, letter writing, even grocery list writing, keep surfaces clear to allow yourself space for these items. By giving everything that resides in the living area a home, you're clearing space on surfaces for those temporary items to stay while in use. By designating a spot for each object, you'll be able to easily tidy up before you even leave the room.

The living area is one room where a 5 minute decluttering session should be done daily. With its many uses, it's inevitable that by the end of the day, there's more mess than in other rooms. Taking a few minutes to return items to the rooms they belong will cut down on the overall clutter in the space. This makes it easy to focus on cleaning for impending guests and to meet your own cleaning schedule.

Floors: Floors in the living area are subject to every kind of dirt and dust buildup from supporting the life that happens within. There are a few ways you can get ahead of that dirt and dust while lessening the burden of cleaning the floors. Start with your entryway. Implement a shoe storage and organization system that will cut down on dirt in the rest of your home by trapping it near the door. Use a low pile rug in the entry to capture small particles of dirt.

Even with diligence at the front door, the living area can quickly collect dirt, dust, and hair tracked in from across the house. Carpet is an easy way to obscure dirt until you can vacuum, but hard flooring like wood or vinyl can be easier to clean when spills happen. A happy medium is a hard flooring with an area rug or two. The rugs will help capture all the dust, dirt, and hair to keep the floor cleaner between vacuuming. If drinks spill on the rug, you can spot clean. If the spot is beyond the cleaners you have at home, it should be taken in to be cleaned professionally.

I recommend rugs even if you are working with a carpeted area. Tastefully selected runners and other area rugs can help cut down on deep stains on your carpet from spills or high traffic. They can even be useful when needing to conceal stains you've spot cleaned, but will need to deep clean with a professional machine. This is especially important in a vacation rental living space. If you're experiencing a high volume of guests, there may not be enough time to professionally clean your carpet after a guest spills something. In a case where you must check in another guest before tending to the carpet, rugs offer a quick temporary solution. This will help keep your guests pleased with the appearance of your space without the need to alter reservations to do so. Always spot clean any carpet before a new guest arrives. If you make it the first on your cleaning list for turning over the space, there will be ample time to see if it is effective.

As for cleaning floors, make the most of your time by starting in one high traffic spot and working your way into the room going from one side of the other and back. Vacuuming or sweeping this way is similar to the difference between the two popular brands of robotic vacuums found in homes today. The Shark® brand robotic vacuum programs a pattern into a robot that operates until it reaches an obstacle before turning another direction. The final pattern looks something like the pattern of a 1990's screensaver where the software logo bounced around the screen. The iRobot Roomba® robotic vacuum performs its function in a simple up and down pattern. If the tray fills up halfway through a room, you know exactly where it stops. Similar with your vacuuming and sweeping, if you're called away in the middle of your work, you know exactly where you left off when you utilize an up and down pattern.

Speaking of robotic vacuums, I do appreciate their utility and would recommend them to certain households. They are an expensive cleaning tool, especially since they cannot completely replace your old vacuum. You will still need something to be able to grab quickly to clean when there is a time crunch. The cycle of the robotic vacuum often requires more time than you have (especially if you're pressed for it). I suggest this as an optional tool, as opposed to a must-have. In addition, the point of this book is not about filling your cleaning closet with expensive gadgets, but helping you keep your house cleaning under control.

Cleaning For Unexpected Guests (15 min):

When unexpected guests are en route, the part of your living area that probably scares you the most is the clutter. This includes snacks left out after watching a movie the night before, opened mail piling up and laundry waiting to be folded. All of this can be handled swiftly to allow yourself a few minutes to sweep or vacuum the floor.

Start with paper: Walk around the living space and gather all of the paper in sight. This includes magazines, mail, flyers and everything that is flat. Stack all paper neatly together in a corner of the room. If you really don't want any of it out, you can relocate it to another room temporarily. However, that often leads to important papers being lost and lessens the chance of you dealing with the stack when guests leave.

Organize the clutter: Perhaps you were doing a home manicure and left all your tools out. Maybe you had your camera and its cleaning kit out to perform maintenance. Whatever clutter you have left out on surfaces, arrange it so it looks like it belongs there. The aesthetic difference between a camera cleaning kit being strewn onto a coffee table and pieces of the same kit laid out in perfect symmetry is quite enormous. Like with paper, it's important to keep these items close at hand in the space. Taking part in the system of stacking clutter away behind closed doors does little to help your overall goal of a cleaner and more tidy home.

Take care of the trash: Since living areas are for meant for living, trash is inevitable. Take the snack wrapper left behind and the junk mail piled on the side table to their proper home. Glance next to and behind furniture for any trash you may have missed.

Focus on the floors: Dust on surfaces is a byproduct of living that doesn't pronounce itself as loudly as dirt on floors. In an effort to have the greatest impact on a living space in a short period of time, focus on the floors. If the vacuum doesn't stand a chance of getting taken out and put away in time, grab the broom and sweep. If you have carpet and thus need the vacuum, focus on high traffic areas first before moving to other parts of the room.

Whether announced or forgotten about, guests will first take notice of the aesthetic organization of your living space. They are not going to be concerned with why you didn't put your manicure kit away or why they must look at a stack of paper. They're going to see the clean lines and organization first and foremost. While the empty space of coffee and side tables may present a spotless image, they can't spark conversation like the contents of your letter writing kit or the tools for cleaning a camera.

Embrace the fact that your life cannot be completely concealed. It is your home after all, the space in which you live a good part of your life. At the end of the day, guests are here for you, not a spotless space that fell out of a magazine.

Clean by surface:

Upholstery: Upholstery fabric found on furniture and even throw pillows is woven to withstand much more than the clothes fabric. The newest upholstered furniture even mixes in technology to boost the life and durability of its fabric. Many upholstered fabrics contain threads and compounds to block water, similar to a raincoat. There are fabrics whose dyes are meant to withstand years of spot cleaning without losing their complexion. When it comes to cleaning upholstery, it's important to first arm yourself with knowledge about the fabric.

Most upholstery fabrics will be able to withstand the chemicals from a spot cleaner. Nevertheless, make sure you test a small inconspicuous area with the product before using on the rest of the upholstery. Fabrics like silk and velvet require additional caution and should be cleaned by professionals. For fabrics made of cotton and synthetics, a store bought stain remover from a brand like Woolite® will be engineered to safely remove stains. Use a soft cloth and follow the directions on the bottle.

If you're looking to simply spruce up your upholstery rather than tackle a specific stain, a simple fabric spray can be used. Fill a spray bottle with 1 cup white vinegar and 3 cups water. Mist over the upholstery without soaking it. The vinegar will lift scents left behind by removing them from the upholstery.

If the lifestyle in your home involves pets and children, consider investing in upholstered furniture with removable covers. Stylish and beautiful furniture can also be easy to keep clean when it utilizes removable covers. Machine wash these fabrics according to their label.

Furniture: To help prevent furniture from getting dirty, you can implement a few items into your lifestyle. Coasters for drinks are helpful for wood furniture as well as furniture made of other materials. Custom cut glass tops can also prolong the surface of furniture, wooden or otherwise. Even without custom glass, you can utilize textiles appropriate to your decor to act as a protective layer between furniture and spills.

For cleaning all furniture and making it last, take a damp cloth and wipe down tops, sides, legs, and feet. By running over every inch of your furniture with this soft cloth, you're able to capture all of the dirt and dust built up. For everyday cleaning of wood furniture, use only a soft cloth. You can boost the shine of the wood with wax cleaners, but they leave a film behind. After the film accumulates, the initial purpose of the wax cleaner is lost on the build-up.

Living areas are often the most used rooms in homes and the most visible to guests. Their importance can inspire you to focus more on the decor in a living room than other rooms in your home. Consider looking at your decor from the perspective of cleaning, rather than strictly expressing your own style. Ask yourself what could be moved or eliminated completely to cut down on your cleaning time. You may forego placing any decorative items on the floor to speed up the floor cleaning process. Perhaps you decide to express your style in larger objects rather than smaller ones because they're easier to dust. It's easy to meld your taste with an easy to clean living area.

This chapter empowers you with the knowledge and techniques to create and maintain a clean space in your living area. This is hugely impactful on your state of mind and well-being because living areas are often the first space you see when arriving home. They can also hold so much meaning due to their role as a setting for our lives. Living areas host parties with friends, quiet solitude with a good book, and much more. Keeping it clean may offer a positive impression to visiting guests, but it can have the most impact on you and the life you bring to it.

Chapter 7: Bedrooms

Bedrooms are a sanctuary within the home where rest and relaxation should take precedence. If you live in a studio apartment, your bedroom may also be part of the living and dining area. If you have roommates, you may keep a TV in your room to allow for separate relaxation. It may be the only space for your home office and thus needs to be supportive of your working mind (not to mention, your resting mind). Even if you only use your bedroom for sleep, you're spending a large amount of time in one room of your home. Cleaning and keeping it that way is supportive of your entire day. Getting the best sleep in a clean environment, powers your entire day.

As important as a clean bedroom is to your life, it can be easy for your schedule to get in the way and cause you to shut the door on the mess. When that happens, use the cleaning tasks and times below to help get you back on track. They're perfect for maintaining a clean bedroom in the time available to you. The following increments and tasks can be combined with other house cleaning tasks to be most efficient.

10 minutes:

Make bed: One of the fastest ways to improve the look of your bedroom is by making your bed. If you have a second set of bed linens, there's even time to switch everything out in less than 10 minutes. If there's anything on the bed prior to making it up, take a minute to put everything away in its proper place.

Fold laundry: If the state of your bed is less unkempt and more covered in fresh laundry, sit down and take 10 minutes to fold and put it away. Setting a timer for 10 minutes and committing to folding and putting it away is the perfect solution for the multi-step process of clothes laundering.

20 minutes:

Vacuum floors: Pick up any clutter and vacuum every inch of the floor. If you have area rugs, shake them out or put them in the washer to start a cycle. If there's time leftover, deal with the clutter you picked up by returning it to its home, wherever in the house that may be.

Remove clutter: Starting from the top and working your way down, clear all your surfaces of clutter. If you don't have time to put everything away, at least arrange everything neatly so that the aesthetic comprises clean lines rather than disjointed piles of objects. Give special attention to your nightstand to ensure its continued functionality for you.

30 minutes:

Wipe down surfaces: In 30 minutes, you can wipe down all surfaces and sides. Starting with the tallest piece of furniture, take a damp cloth and wipe down the top before moving to the sides and legs. Move on to shorter pieces, like nightstands or headboards. Don't forget about mirrors or windows. Clear up the reflective surface on both with a soft cloth and a bit of window cleaner.

Return items: Gather the items around your bedroom that belong elsewhere in your home. Take the time to put them precisely where they belong, not just anywhere in the room they reside. Taking time to do this not only declutters your bedroom, but helps support the overall cleanliness of your home.

The following check points need special attention in the bedroom, even if you neglect them in other parts of your home. They all directly affect the quality of your sleep and overall liveability of the room.

Clean air:

Clean air is vital to the place where you spend so much of your time. Investing in an air purifier will ensure the air you breathe during every REM cycle is clean. You can modify your existing HVAC system to include various types of filters that work differently from the standard filters. This will affect the air throughout your home rather than just your bedroom. Because these modifications can be more costly than purchasing a one-room purifier, they require more financial planning to achieve. For now, a standalone air purifier will achieve the desired result.

In order to remove mold, allergens and other pollutants from your air, you would need multiple types of air purifiers (and even a dehumidifier) running at the same time. The maintenance alone for all of these machines could take up a half-day of cleaning time. The best solution is to identify the needs unique to your health and your space. Different types of air purifier filters are good at pulling different things out of the air.

Types of air purifier filters:

HEPA filters: High Efficiency Particulate Air or HEPA is a type of filter meant to pull dust and other allergens out of the air. It can catch particulates of varying sizes and is completely sealed, meaning those particulates won't escape again. You will need to replace the filter on a regular basis, as it cannot be cleaned and reused.

Ionizer: Ionizer purifiers work by sending out negative ions into your space that latch onto positively charged ions, which includes allergens, dust and bacteria. These particles are then trapped by the purifier.

Most air purifiers that have an ionizer also have a HEPA filter to help filter more out of the air. The effectiveness of the ionizer will depend on how frequently you dust and vacuum. Since the negative ions going out don't always make it back through the filter, they end up on positively charged surfaces in the room and floor. This is acceptable if you vacuum and dust on a regular basis, but something to be mindful of.

UV filters: UV light can attract bacteria and mold in the air trapping it. Unfortunately, in order to be effective they draw on more power and can't trap the UV-resistant bacteria in the air.

An air purifier with a HEPA filter provides a happy medium wherein dust and particles are trapped while maintaining the machine is as simple as replacing a filter. If your bedroom is subject to mold because of the climate you're in or the placement of the room in your home, consider investing in a dehumidifier that allows you to control the humidity. You can keep the humidity at a comfortable level without spurring on mold growth in your space.

Other ways to keep your air clean include dusting, regular bedding changes, and preventing dirt from entering your room. You should dust your bedroom every week, even if dusting in other rooms falls out of your schedule.

You should also change your bedding at least once a week. Showering before bed can help cut down on dust and allergens that build up in your bedding over the course of a week. If you have curtains in your bedroom, launder them regularly, about once a month. If the fabric is not machine washable, use your dust attachment for your vacuum to clean them once a month.

Clean aesthetics:

One way to help support a cleaner environment in your bedroom is by removing unnecessary clutter from view. Put aside the bottles of perfume, pieces of jewelry, and other accessories as forms of decor. Instead, opt for pieces that fit into the design of your bedroom space and reflect you. To keep the useful items close at hand, utilize the storage already found in the room, dresser drawers and shelves.

Due to the proximity of your bedroom to the bathroom, you may find yourself surrounded by piles of clean and dirty laundry. Luckily, there is a simple solution to eliminating the clutter. Find decorative baskets that can hold clean laundry before you've had a chance to fold it and put it away. Keep a second basket for dirty clothes to keep your bedroom clutter down. It's easy to transfer the dirty clothes from the decorative basket to the laundry basket. This process allows you to quickly sort your laundry on the spot. Look for decorative baskets with handles that provide portability and find a style that includes a lid for additional concealment.

Hidden spaces:

It's often the hidden spaces that contain the most dirt and dust in your bedroom. Furniture like dressers and beds often are designed with decorative legs raising them off the floor. The aesthetic is a pleasing one, but it means you'll need to be diligent about vacuuming under these pieces regularly. Even carpeted bedrooms have a buildup of dirt under furniture. Use vacuum attachments to reach as much as you can under furniture during routine vacuuming. If some spaces still prove difficult to reach, arrange to move furniture every few months to vacuum.

It's easy to shut the door to your bedroom and focus on the cleanliness in the rest of your home. In doing so, you end up neglecting one of the most sacred rooms. Your bedroom is a sanctuary, a place where you can rest and recharge. If you can keep its use to these purposes, you'll have a space that's easy to care for and keep clean.

Chapter 8: Bathrooms

The bathrooms in your home are some of the most important spaces to keep clean. Due to the nature of their use, they often contain more germs and bacteria than other spaces in your house. It's important to establish a cleaning routine for the bathroom that you can keep up with, even when life gets busy. To help you reset to a base level of clean, I've put together a number of different cleaning tasks organized by the time it takes to complete them. When it's the end of a long day and tomorrow is looking busier, you can pull out a task or two and take care of them immediately. This puts you in a cleaner position as you take on the remaining tasks the following day.

10 minutes:

Clear surfaces: Remove any clutter from countertops, shelves, and other surfaces. Return toiletries to where they belong and throw any trash away. Pick up any dirty laundry from the floor.

Wipe everything down: If clutter is not your obstacle, but dried toothpaste in the sink basin has you blocked, take 10 minutes and wipe everything down, including mirrors. Using a soft cloth and an all-purpose cleaner safe for your bathroom surfaces, wipe down the faucet, sink, and countertops. Then move on to the back of the toilet, the toilet seat, and the top of the toilet bowl. If there's time left over, take out your bathroom trash and replace the bag so it's ready for guests.

20 minutes:

Floors: Put your bath mats in the laundry and clear the floor of anything else before vacuuming or sweeping. Dry mop for an even deeper clean before laying out your cleaned bath mats.

Focus on sinks and toilets: By focusing on making the sinks and toilet shine in your bathroom, you're creating a focal point of clean for guests. Start with the toilet. Using your favorite disinfecting cleaner and a soft cloth, wipe down the toilet from top to bottom. Make sure you wipe down the entire outside of the toilet basin and get into the tight corners of the toilet's base. Gather your deep cleaning tools and finish at the sink. These tools include a toothbrush or similarly sized cleaning brush, your favorite sink cleaner, and a soft cloth.

Spray the faucet with the cleaner and let sit while you wipe the basin. Taking your toothbrush, scrub the faucet to remove any water spots, soap buildup, and other grime dulling the shine.

30 Minutes:

Focus on fixtures: Dusting a towel bar isn't the first thing that comes to mind when cleaning the bathroom, but it can be an important task in achieving a high standard of clean. Take account of all the fixtures in your bathroom, including any visible storage like decorative baskets or art hanging on the wall. Starting with the fixtures that are highest up, wipe down everything with a soft damp cloth. For items like decorative baskets, empty their contents, then hold the basket upside down over a trash can and brush out any dirt in the bottom with a dry toothbrush. For any bathroom art, assess the material and then use either a dry duster or a soft damp cloth to clean it. Replace any towels that were on towel bars and use this time to also put away any clothes hanging on bathroom hooks.

45 minutes:

Grout cleaning: Using a paste of bleach and baking soda, layer the lines of grout with cleaner. You can also use a store bought grout cleaner for this task.

Wait 15 minutes before returning with a toothbrush or similarly sized cleaning brush to scrub at each line of grout. Rinse with a wet damp cloth, making sure to rinse out the cloth regularly. Use your favorite tile cleaner on the entire surface of tile and grout to give it a polished look. A shower itself could take about 45 minutes, so decide if you're going to focus on the floor grout or shower grout.

If you have more than one bathroom, and you don't have a lot of time, mix and match the tasks above to achieve the same look in each bathroom.

If you have 30 minutes and 3 bathrooms, employ the decluttering cleaning task to bring them up to the same level of clean.

Daily bathroom habits:

Between bouts of cleaning, there are daily habits you can adopt to help support a guest-ready bathroom at all times. As with any new habit, it will take time to build them into your routine. I recommend starting with one habit for a week to feel the difference in your space. As that habit begins to establish itself in your routine, add another.

Habit #1: Pick up clothes

It's easy to let clothes pile up just outside the shower. It seems especially easy right after cleaning the bathroom when the floors are so fresh and sanitized. Make a point of getting any clothes that come off your body right into your hamper. If your bathroom is too small to keep a hamper, consider a small basket that can either hang on the towel rack or sit neatly under the sink to catch the day's clothes. Whichever way you choose, make sure it lessens the burden of putting clothes away and doesn't complicate it.

Habit #2: Find homes for products

As you integrate new products into your daily care routine, you should also incorporate a place for them to live. If your shower is separate from the rest of your bathroom, you might consider keeping lotion and face moisturizer within your shower to maximize counter space. If you tend to do your makeup in your bedroom, but lack storage, you might opt to keep products organized in a bathroom drawer. The products that can be left out should be the ones used on a daily or twice daily basis. Toothbrushes, hair brushes, makeup, shaving products, and facial creams all fall into this category. Choose what you'd like to keep out based on the size of the countertop or storage surface available. If you have a pedestal sink with barely enough room to hold a soap pump, consider a medicine cabinet or over-the-toilet shelving system. Both of these storage solutions will allow you to keep important products close at hand. If you have a large countertop surface surrounding your sink, consider decorative trays to separate sets of products from each other. Keeping them on trays means when it's time to clean, you can pick up the tray, move it, clean the area, and return the tray to its proper home.

With these tips in mind, it is also important to know when your storage is inefficient. If you find your daily routine is interrupted to retrieve a product, then it's being stored in the wrong place.

Habit #3: Use it and store it

When you've found homes for everything, this habit should be easy to adopt. When you use products during your morning and evening routines, return them back to where they belong. The few seconds it takes to open a drawer or cabinet door will save you several minutes when it comes time to clean the bathroom. If your products have packaging to be thrown away after use, make sure there is a trash can nearby.

The Perfect Guest Bathroom:

For guests, you may have a separate powder room with just a toilet and sink. Or perhaps your own bathroom may serve as the defacto guest bathroom. Whatever the case, there are a few simple ways to stock your bathroom so it is always ready for guests. Stock your toilet area with a surface cleaner or air spray guests can easily access if they need to utilize it. For menstruating guest, keep tampons and pads stocked and in plain sight. If you're stocking a bathroom for overnight guests, arrange containers of important tools like cotton balls and cotton tips for easy access. Always keep fresh hand towels and rolls of toilet paper in the bathroom, concealed in a decorative basket or stored under the sink.

Return to Factory Settings Clean:

This section is especially helpful when moving into a new place where "deep clean" was not part of the previous resident's vocabulary. It will also be useful when you wake up one day and realize how much of your daily routine has built up around faucets and drains. Deep cleans like the ones below can be done on an as needed basis. It will depend on the frequency of use the bathroom receives and can't always be scheduled. I recommend completing them as part of your entry into a new era of clean in your home.

Sink:

The pressure points in a sink tend to be the drain itself and the area where the base of the faucet meets the sink. It's easy for soap and other gunk to build up in these places creating a film that's difficult to tackle. Using your favorite deep cleaner or a mix of baking soda with vinegar, apply the cleaner and let sit for 10 minutes. You should cover the drain and the base of the faucet completely with the cleaner. Scrub the areas with a toothbrush or cleaning brush. Next, focus on the faucet itself. Using your favorite all-purpose cleaner, spray the faucet liberally and scrub each corner with the toothbrush. Wipe the cleaner and mess away with a soft cloth and assess any leftover dirt or stains. Repeat the process, if necessary. To give your sink basin a fresh look, use a cleaner safe for the surface and spray liberally. Working in a circular motion with a soft cloth, clean the basin. Use a clean dry soft cloth at the end to polish it up and remove any leftover cleaner residue.

Toilet:

Start from the top and work your way to the bottom. Using your favorite cleaner with disinfectant, clean the top of the toilet tank and work your way down the sides. Be sure to get the lever used to engage flushing. Wipe down the toilet cover, the toilet seat, and the rim of the basin underneath the toilet seat. Remove the toilet seat entirely with a screwdriver or appropriate tool. Set the toilet seat hardware in a large bin soaking in hot water and soap. Using a new soft cloth, scrub the toilet where the seat attached removing any stains hidden by the hardware. Rinse the toilet seat hardware and, if needed, use a paper towel to clean them when the water isn't enough. Spray your disinfectant cleaner on all components after washing in the sink and let dry. Put the seat back on the toilet. Move on to the bottom of the toilet basin wiping with the disinfectant cleaner. Work your way into the base of the toilet and even reach into the small space between the back of the toilet and the wall.

Shower:

Two of the most common types of showers are acrylic and tile. Both have their advantages and both can get to the point where they need a deep clean. If you have an acrylic shower, the first tool you'll need is the Mr. Clean Magic Eraser® or a store brand version of it. Use the eraser to tackle soap scum around the base of the tub and any spots on the walls of the shower. After using the eraser, take your favorite shower cleaner and soak the walls and base. Let sit for five minutes before scrubbing with a brush. Rinse with water and use a squeegee to help dry the surface without leaving spots. If you have a tile shower, most likely with a porcelain or similar tub, find your favorite grout cleaner and apply it to all lines of the grout. While that sits, focus your attention onto the basin or tub. Using a bleach-based cleaner, spray the basin or tub liberally. Once the tub is coated, use a cleaning brush to scrub in a circular motion. Work your way around the tub until you've scrubbed every part. Moving back to the grout, test a small section with your toothbrush to see if the cleaner has sat long enough. If the grout is noticeably different, go ahead and scrub the rest of the grout lines. Rinse the tile and grout with water before spraying your favorite disinfectant cleaner. Use a squeegee on the tile and grout before moving back to the basin or tub. Rinse the tub with hot water before spraying disinfectant cleaner and wiping the tub down.

You want it to be almost completely dry to avoid water spots. At the end of these cleaning techniques, your drain and showerhead should have gotten a clean of their own. If there are still water spots or stains, take a cleaner that can handle calcium, lime, and rust like CLR® and spray these areas. Let sit and then wipe away.

The products used in the deep clean of your bathroom are strong and effective. This also means that they contain chemicals that you may not want to be exposed to on a daily basis. Once your bathroom is cleaned using these products, you will be able to keep ahead of water stains and deep grout stains with your regular cleaning routine. These products should stay on the shelf more than they are used, but are so helpful when the situation warrants it.

Keeping a clean bathroom starts with a few daily habits and ends with a solid cleaning routine. In the middle, there's room for a deep clean that restores the space to its original fresh out-of-the-box state. As with timed tasks for other rooms, you can mix and match the tasks in this chapter.

Mixing them together, you can create a cleaning spree to match available time and the rooms that need attention. Your bathroom can be not only the room in which you prepare yourself for the day but a room frequented by visiting guests. It's easy for the room to fulfill its purposes when cared for properly using the tools and strategies in this chapter.

Chapter 9: Floors

The flooring in your home can be one of the most costly parts of construction and renovation. Even if you didn't foot the bill for the current flooring in your home, the rent or purchase price paid for your house includes the quality of the flooring material. Different types of flooring require different techniques, products, and tools. While there is often crossover in tools and even cleaning products, each material has its own quirks. This chapter breaks down the top flooring materials offering tips and techniques to clean quickly and effectively. In this chapter you will learn that it is possible to a have guest-ready floor merely days after cleaning.

Tile:

Tile is a natural choice for bathrooms and kitchens. In homes with warmer climates, tile is often used throughout the house. The standard material in tiles is ceramic which is then glazed to achieve different finishes. Floor tile is often going to have a glaze with some texture to prevent it from becoming dangerous when wet. The grouts used with floor tile are most likely sanded grout. Unsanded grout is typically reserved for glass tile to prevent scratching the tile surface during application. Tile and grout is easy to maintain and makes spot cleaning a breeze.

The right cleaner for your tile: Most tiles are non-porous and can be cleaned using a homemade cleaner or a store bought cleaner made for tile. One exception is stone tiles such as travertine. Travertine will require a stone cleaner, which can be purchased from your local hardware store or cleaning aisle of you local big box store like Target or Wal-Mart.

Dry cleaning:

There's a number of tools available to keep tile floors clean and their effectiveness depends on the use for the room. For tile in the kitchen, the most effective dry cleaning tool is a broom. A broom will clean up food crumbs of any size while a vacuum may not be able to handle larger pieces of debris. Tile in living areas can benefit from a dust mop that you can easily glide around the room collecting dust and dirt. Any excess can be swept right into a dustpan. In the bathroom, a broom or vacuum will do. If tile dominates your home, a vacuum will be the fastest way to remove dirt and dust.

Spot cleaning: There will inevitably be spots that require more than a once over with a mop. Depending on the spot, you may need to take a cloth wet with hot water and let it sit over the spot to loosen it up. After a few minutes, you can wipe it away.

Wet cleaning: Mopping with a dry mop, like the kit from Bona or a similar one from janitorial supply companies, is the best way to clean tile. When you have a dry mopping kit with multiple pads, you can easily change out a dirty pad for a clean one as you go along. This keeps dirt and germs from spreading around during mopping. Another great tool for tile is a steam mop. It's a happy medium between a traditional mop and a dry mop. You can fill up the tank with water, turn it on, and while waiting for the steam to build up, sweep or vacuum the area of tile. Steam mops also come with reusable pads, so you can change them during cleaning as they get dirty. A dry mop has a much lower buy in compared to the steam mop, but the steam mop cleans floors with no chemicals needed.

Tile sealing:

If installed properly, your grout would have received an application of sealer to deflect stains and signs of heavy use. It is recommended that you seal grout once a year, depending on how much traffic the tile endures. Your local hardware store will offer the sealer you need and the bottle contains instructions for application. In order to prep grout for sealing, reach for a bleach and baking soda paste that can remove even the deepest stains. Once the grout is rinsed of any leftover baking soda and fully dry, the grout is ready for sealing.

Hardwood:

Hardwood is a classic look that can be purchased new or found hiding under carpet and even salvaged from old homes. Caring for wood properly begins with understanding the type of wood used in the flooring. Pine is often a popular choice and cost effective, but it is a soft wood that regular sealing in the form of polyurethane or similar can make up for. Pine has a beautiful look, but care should be taken to protect it from scratches and dents by using area rugs. You can also initiate a no-shoes rule for your pine floors.

Pine is one of the softest woods, but there are many durable types used in flooring. Bamboo, oak, maple, ash, and even mahogany all make up strong hardwood floors. With proper sealing, you can easily clean all types of wood with homemade or store bought cleaners.

Dry Cleaning (Dusting): A soft dry cloth is perfect for gathering dust and debris from your wood floor. If you have a dry mop system to clean your floors, it's easy to change those pads for a soft one to take care of dusting.

Dry Cleaning (Vacuuming): Vacuuming can be a quick way to get dirt off hardwood floors, especially when there's too much for a duster to handle. To keep your floors in top shape, make sure your vacuum has a soft brush attachment. This will not only glide over the floor without scratching, it will also pick up hair and other fine particles ensuring they're trapped.

Spot cleaning: When there's a few drops of coffee or the results of your cat's sensitive stomach resting on your hardwood floors, reach for your favorite hardwood cleaner. Spray a little onto the spot and then begin your dry mopping process. By the time you get to the spot, it will come up easily.

Wet cleaning: A dry mop kit works well for hardwood and allows you to have a system that works in rooms with tile in addition to hardwood. Use a favorite hardwood cleaner and change the pads regularly to keep from dragging dirt around the floor. If your hardwood is older and lacks the strong seal of newer hardwood, you may want to use a floor wax like Minwax® or Old English® brand floor wax. These products not only clean, but leave behind a layer of wax as protection for the floor.

Protecting floors: Even with proper sealing, hardwood is subject to damage from furniture, shoes, and accidents. Take care with a few preventative measures and ensure the longevity of your floors. All furniture resting on hardwood should be outfitted with soft furniture pads on the points of contact with the floor. If you have any houseplants resting on the wood floor, make sure they have trays under them to collect any excess water that drains out of the pot. If there is water or pet damage that goes undetected, even the best sealants can be compromised. If this happens, you may need your floor professionally patched. For reasons like these, it's important to hold onto any leftover materials after a floor install.

Laminate:

Laminate is becoming a popular choice for flooring in kitchens, bathrooms, living areas, and even bedrooms. The technology for laminate has advanced to where it can look like hardwood or even plank tile. It's highly durable and able to withstand heavy wear and tear in kitchens as well as living areas. The maintenance of laminate is easy and the price is more affordable than hardwood or tile. In the kitchen, it provides the perfect blend of hardwood and tile. It's soft like hardwood making it easier to stand on for long periods but has the durability of tile when a dish is dropped or shoes are worn on it.

Dry cleaning: With varying textures of laminate, a vacuum is the best tool for picking up dirt and debris. You can use a soft brush attachment on your vacuum like you would with hardwood. This makes it easier to go room to room with the same equipment if you have multiple floor types in your home. A vacuum will grab all dust and dirt out of laminate efficiently without worrying about leaving anything behind.

Spot cleaning: Even with its durability, laminate is not meant to withstand abrasive cleaners. Instead, rely on the dry mop pads to work on tough spots and get into every space of the laminate surface. When those won't work, a plastic bristle brush is perfect for getting rid of a spot ahead of mopping.

Wet cleaning: Dry mop systems come with pads, often made of microfiber or longer loomed cotton, that will pick up dirt easily from any texture of laminate. You can use a favorite homemade cleaner or buy one made for laminate. There are even cleaners safe for both laminate and hardwood, cutting down on the number of products you need if you have multiple floor types in your home.

Carpets:

The variety of carpet types available creates a multitude of approaches to cleaning for one floor type. Low-pile carpet typically does not hold onto dirt and dust as easily as high-pile carpet. There's carpet specifically made for high-traffic areas that is not only low-pile, but tightly loomed to prevent tears or snags as well as repel dirt. Carpet is often the obvious choice to add warmth to a room, such as finished basements and bedrooms.

Dry cleaning: Vacuuming is the easiest way to get your carpets clean. To make sure you're getting the most out of the time spent vacuuming carpet, there's a few things to check on the vacuum itself. Make sure the brush is not wound completely with fibers and hairs. If it is, take a pair of scissors to begin cutting off the mess in sections. Make sure there is a new bag or the canister is completely empty before vacuuming. You don't want to have to empty the canister halfway through vacuuming and any dirt left in it will impede the machine's ability to collect more dirt. Make sure the filters are cleaned or replaced on a regular basis. A clogged filter will affect the suction of the vacuum. Make sure you adjust the brush height to match your carpet. If you have low-pile carpet, adjust it to a lower setting so it sits closer to the carpet itself. If you have high-pile, adjust it up so it sits far enough above the fibers to capture all dirt and dust as the brush spins.

Spot cleaning: The approach will be determined by the type of spot to be tackled. If a pet has an accident, you're not only dealing with a surface spot but anything that has drifted to the pad or subfloor below. Test an inconspicuous area first, but apply white vinegar liberally to the urine or feces stain. Then, sprinkle baking soda liberally over the spot. Cover with a laundry basket or similar to keep from walking on it and let dry for a few days. For non-pet stains, it's easy to keep a store bought cleaner on hand and follow the directions to remove the stain. Remember that a stain is easier to remove when it is still wet, so as soon as it happens, grab the cleaner and take care of it.

Wet cleaning: Depending on the volume of traffic on your carpet, wet cleaning should be done sparingly. Once a year or every other year will work depending on the volume of traffic. Refer back to the recipes chapter for a homemade concentrate to use in professional carpet cleaners. Store bought is fine, too, but homemade will save a little money.

Other flooring types:

Marble: Marble is porous and thus susceptible to stains without proper protection. Use a marble specific cleaner and avoid letting the cleaner dry on the marble. Always wipe up the cleaner and use a soft microfiber cloth to avoid scratches to the marble.

Stone: The extent of stone flooring in your home may be the fireplace hearth, but some homes have stone as flooring in other parts, as well. Stone, like travertine tile, can be porous and care should be taken not to leave liquids resting on it to dry. Wiping it down with a vinegar cleaner will remove everyday dirt and dust. If needed, scrubbing with a plastic bristle brush can help break up tough dirt.

It's not often that a home will have just one type of flooring throughout. Rather than let the various needs of flooring types fill utility closets with tools and cleaners, invest in items that can perform multiple functions. A vacuuming and mopping system that can go from tile to hardwood and then to laminate will make the job go by much faster. Vacuums that can transform quickly into the perfect dirt buster on carpet before gently taking up dust on hard flooring make the job less stressful. There are ways to cut down on the dirt and dust entering your house, but at the end of the day, your floors play catchall for your entire home. Find the right tools for your home and the task of keeping floors clean will become easier and more enjoyable.

Chapter 10: Additional Areas

The preceding chapters covered the rooms that take up the most space in your home and thus require the most detail for cleaning and upkeep. In this chapter, I'm sharing the proven strategies to keeping all the other spaces in your home immaculate. Garages, entryways, laundry rooms, and closets fill in the space around your larger living areas. While some are used exclusively for storage, others see high-foot traffic and use on a daily basis. Maintaining each space will help support your efforts to keep the rest of your home clean. They might be able to provide a quick getaway for clutter when guests drop in last minute. They might keep all your cleaning products organized and tidy motivating you in your mission to keep house. Each space has a purpose and keeping it clean means it can fulfill that purpose to the fullest extent.

Closets:

Your home most likely has at least one clothes closet and one linen closet (while some homes have a separate coat closet and utility closet). Altogether, closets are the secret ingredients to keeping a home clean. Without them, clothes, shoes, linens, and more would be strewn everywhere or crammed into furniture wardrobes taking up extra space. Depending on the type of closet, there are a few strategies to keep these spaces clean.

Clothes closets: Whether you have a walk-in closet big enough to fit an area rug or a standard depth closet with a simple clothes bar, it can get messy quickly. Forgotten clothes fall back behind stored suitcases while the floor completely misses vacuuming because it's closed off and out of mind. With the fibers from clothes both dirty and clean, it's important to dust your closet from top to bottom on a regular basis. A microfiber duster works perfectly well and can fit around every ring of an open shelf.

Part of cleaning your clothes closet is decluttering. Having less in the space means less dust created and an easier time cleaning the space. When decluttering, make sure you have the adequate storage containers for what's in your closet. Proper storage solutions keep contents fresh and ready to use at a moment's notice. Plastic bins in varying sizes offer transparent views to see contents while baskets with lids let items breathe. Baskets are great for sweaters and clothes while bins hold books, sports equipment and travel accessories.

When decluttering and organizing your closet, keep the floor open as possible. This will ensure that when you are vacuuming the room just outside, you can quickly cover the closet floor by simply opening the doors. It's easy for dust and dirt to get trapped in closet floors, especially if they're carpet.

Linen closets: Linen closets can quickly become the messiest room in a house due to their contents and use of those items. Sheets and blankets fall to the floor when you try to grab a specific set. Floors can become covered in dust from the linens themselves. In order to keep the linen closet cleaner for longer, invest in storage that you can label. Store all linens categorically making it easy to find what you need.

If you have solid shelves, wipe them down with a soft cloth and and an all-purpose cleaner once a month. If you have wire shelves, a microfiber duster works well. Keep floors as open as possible to make it easy to vacuum or sweep. Many linen closets perform double-duty storing linens as well as cleaners and other tools. If this is the case in your closet, pay special attention to where you store each item. Cleaners should all be stored below linens. This prevents accidental spills onto fabrics and offers the floor to land on. If you have small children in the home and are worried about cleaners being in reach, invest in a child lock for the linen closet door. Utilize the space on the back of the linen closet door to store tools like brooms and dusters. Depending on the depth of the closet, you may also be able to fit a vacuum in the space as well.

Storage closets: If a home lacks a garage space, there is often a storage closet to make up for it. They're used to hold tools, sporting equipment, and anything else that isn't used in the home itself. This area should have its own set of tools for cleaning to keep outside dirt from being brought into the home. A stiff bristle broom for sweeping is a must. They can easily be found at your local hardware store (sometimes described as a shop or industrial broom).

If you have solid shelves in the storage area, keep them dust free by wiping them down with a wet soft cloth either monthly or bi-monthly. The frequency will depend on the season and how often the items in storage are being used and put back. Utilize plastic storage bins for items in this area to make them easier to clean when they collect dust.

Pantry closets: A pantry closet should be on your schedule when vacuuming the room surrounding it. As for cleaning, it's good to go through the pantry every 3 months and get rid of expired food. In doing so, you can also reorganize what you have making it easier to see what's available. Wipe shelves from top to bottom before sweeping the floor and mopping it with your dry mop system.

Laundry Room:

The most frequent cleaning need I've found in laundry rooms is dusting. The clothes dryer is almost always in use and the filter cleaned out between every load. This allows for many particulates to make their way into the air and settle onto surfaces. To help cut down on dust from the lint trap, keep a lidded trash can close to the dryer. When it comes to cleaning the rest of the laundry room, start with any exposed surfaces like shelves and the outside of your washer and dryer. Take time to clean out the lint trap using your vacuum hose. A full cleaning of the dryer duct should be conducted every 3 months or so, depending on the volume of usage.

To clean inside your washer, begin by cleaning out the washing machine filter. Depending on how full it is, there may be some water that leaks onto the ground when removing. Keep a towel close by just in case. Then, use the wash setting on your washer or fill the detergent dispenser with white vinegar. In newer washers, throw in a few towels so they are able to sense clothing, provide enough water and put them through a hot wash cycle. Once you've finished cleaning the rest of the room, vacuum or sweep the floor and mop. Wash or vacuum any area rugs used in the space before putting them back down.

Mudrooms and Entryways:

Mudrooms and entryways should contain many of the same tools to keep dirt from going further into your home. Mudrooms tend to be more concealed from the rest of your home while entryways bring you right into the heart of the house. In both settings, proper shoe storage will help keep dirt manageable. Find a system that allows for dirt to collect under where the shoes sit. A wire shelf with a tray underneath accomplishes this goal.

The shelves can be cleaned and dusted so that all dirt and debris is knocked onto the tray below it. The tray can then be dumped into the trash after collecting all the dirt. Find a machine washable rug to keep right at the entryway collecting dirt and dust. With several copies of a machine washable rug, you can change it out a few times a week keeping the area clean. Being able to change out the rug at a moment's notice is what keeps your home guest ready at all times.

Door handles and the doors themselves get a lot of wear and tear. Take care of scuffs from shoes with a Mr. Clean® Magic Eraser. Regularly wipe down the door handle and the area around it to keep dirt from building up and discoloring the area. You can also invest in a decorative toe kick to fit at the base of the door and take the brunt of accidental bumps with shoes and other items going in and out of the door.

Garage:

The main area of concern in a garage is the floor. Leaves, dirt, and trash can easily pile up all over the space. Using an industrial broom, also known as a shop broom, you can sweep the area quickly collecting dirt and trash. Keep a trash can in the garage to avoid temptation to leave it behind or track more dirt into the house looking for a receptacle. If you park your vehicle in the garage, use old cardboard to collect any leaking car fluids keeping the floor clean.

Outdoor Spaces:

Similar to the garage, outdoor spaces will be subject to the whims of mother nature when it comes to dirt buildup. There will also be more spiderwebs and insect homes competing for the space. Depending on whether your outdoor area is decking or a stone patio, there are different ways to keep it clean.

Decks: Wood and synthetic wood decks have several options for keeping the dirt and dust off. One tool to handle it all is a wide industrial broom that can reach between boards due to its weight and operation. There's no need to pick it up and sweep like a traditional broom. Simply set it on the surface and guide it from one end to the other until the entire area has been swept. Choosing this option means you'll need to move deck furniture as you sweep. If that's not feasible, consider an electric leaf blower. With less immediate air pollution than gas leaf blowers, an electric leaf blower can be quickly adjusted on the go. You can increase the power to remove tough piles of wet leaves or needles. You can decrease it as you dislodge dirt from under furniture.

Even with adjustable settings, there is risk of getting dirt on deck furniture cushions. It's safest to remove them before operating the leaf blower to keep them in shape. Water is also an effective tool for a deep clean of your deck but one that should be used sparingly to conserve the resource. Pressure washing is especially useful when preparing to re-stain a deck. Save the water method for instances like that and use one of the other tools for more frequent cleanings. A deck should be cleaned every other week during its busy season.

Patios: The same cleaning schedule applies to patios, although the cleaning methods vary. If you have a patio made with closely knit pavers, a large industrial broom such as the one recommended for decks will work well. An electric leaf blower will also suit. If your patio is a loose gathering of pavers or stones with smaller gravel between each piece, cleaning will need to be more delicate. Dedicate a household-grade broom for your patio to sweep excess fill gravel from patio paver or stones.

For spider webs and other animal homes, try to leave as much as you can intact. If necessary, you can clear door entries and windows while leaving other webs and nests in higher or lower places intact. For a natural repellant that will not harm spiders and other small insects but encourage them to relocate elsewhere, find hybrid plants at your local nursery. Different plants are bred to include the scents of herbs, such as basil, that naturally repel spiders. It's important to support spiders especially because they help keep the outdoors clean and free from bothersome insects like mosquitoes. Depending on where you live, bats will also show up in the outdoor space around your home. If you prefer them to live in another area, invest in an inviting cedar bat house they can migrate to. Believe it or not, bats are wonderful animals that help keep the number of insects down making your outdoor spaces more enjoyable.

I imagine that when you picked up this book you didn't expect to read a section praising the cleaning abilities of spiders and bats. Insights like that are exactly why this book was written. There are so many areas in your home and each requires its own set of rules for cleaning. Tools and techniques often cross over from room to room. Oftentimes, there are specific insights that won't come up in just any old search engine. This chapter captured all the small spaces that weave themselves throughout larger living areas. With plenty of technique crossover and handy tips for specific pressure points, you're ready to get these areas clean and primed for repeated use.

Chapter 11: 7 Day Cleaning Plan

Day 1: Remove Surface Clutter

Depending on the state of your home, there is going to be a lot of clutter taking up space on surfaces all over the house. That's okay. This week is about slowly breaking up that clutter and the dirt that lurks within so cleaning becomes easier and quicker. Like each day during this cleaning week, start one load of laundry and move it to the dryer. The load can be started right at the beginning of the hour and then moved to the dryer at the end.

With this day's hour, tackle the surfaces throughout your home. For convenience, you may want to use a small trash can to carry from room to room.

Bathroom

Countertop:
1. Remove any trash from the countertop or sink vanity
2. Corral products into one place on the countertop, opening up space around them
3. Alternatively, return products to their proper home on shelves or inside a medicine or storage cabinet

Shelves:
1. Remove any trash
2. Bring products together in one place on the shelf, opening up space around them

Floor:
- Pick up any clothes or trash that may have fallen

Kitchen

Counters:
1. Return food to the pantry or other storage space
2. Move dirty dishes to the sink
3. Return tools to their storage space

Shelves:
1. If your kitchen has exposed shelves for storage, remove everything that does not normally live there and move it to its proper storage space
2. Organize shelf contents to be together on one end of the shelf

Floor:
1. Pick up any food wrappers or other trash
2. Return footstools or other kitchen and cleaning tools to their proper storage space

Bedroom

Furniture tops:
1. Remove any clothing that can be worn again before washing and put in a hamper or designated spot.
2. Group together any accessories that normally stay on surface tops. For bedside tables, groupings include lamps and alarm clocks. For dresser tops, this may include watch and cases for eyewear.

Bed:
1. Remove any clothes, books and magazines. Store clothes in hamper. Stack books and magazines neatly on a side table.
2. Make your bed if it isn't already made

Floor:
1. Pick up any clutter from the floor
2. Return items to their homes if they're close by
3. If not, stack them neatly on a dresser, nightstand, or other furniture surface

Living Area

Furniture tops:
1. Remove any trash
2. Organize clutter into groups. Stack books, magazines, and mail together

Shelves:
- Remove any items that do not belong. If their home is close by, return them. Otherwise, stack them neatly on shelves to open up the space around them.

Floor:
1. Pick up shoes, blankets, or any other clutter. Stack them neatly in groups.
2. Fold blankets together on the couch.
3. Move shoes together in a row by the wall or returned to them to their mudroom racks

Other Areas:

These areas include the entryway, mudroom, closets and laundry room. Surface tops may include furniture, machines, display shelves and storage racks

1. Remove any trash from surface tops
2. In the entryway or mudroom, store keys and other items in their proper place or group them together in a basket
3. In the laundry room, return all detergents and laundry supplies to their proper place getting rid of empty containers
4. In the closet, take any dirty clothing to the hamper to be washed and return any clean clothing to hangers or drawers
5. In all areas, organize the remaining items in a group to open up space around them

Floor:

1. Move shoes, coats, books, and any other clutter to surface tops either in the space or the proper storage area for the items
2. Stack shoes in the entryway shoe organizer or the floor
3. Place any books back onto shelves in the living area
4. Hang coats found on chairs in the entryway or closet
5. Pick up any loose socks or other clothing in the laundry room and sort to be washed or put away
6. Shake out rugs in the entryway or mudroom
7. Pick up any clothing or shoes on closet floors and put them where they belong. Move shoes to their organizer. Place clothes in a hamper or hang up.

The key on this day is to touch almost every surface in your home in one hour working from the top to the bottom. Grouping items together to take up less space is intentional. You're setting yourself up for the next step in cleaning without tearing apart shelves and surface tops. At the end of the hour, you may not end up with all the shoes in the home delivered to the shoe rack, but you will have stacked all your shoes in neat groupings. This provides a positive aesthetic versus the chaos of shoes scattered around a room. The mental boost from seeing something like a clean line of shoes will encourage you to continue your progress the next day.

Day 2: Kitchen and Bathrooms Surfaces

The next step can be a little time consuming so it is conveniently broken up into two days. On this day, you're going to wipe down or dust surfaces in both the kitchen and the bathroom. The work you did to declutter the day before has prepared you for this. Items have been grouped together on surface tops so you can immediately clean an area, move the items, and clean the other parts. With no clutter to trip over, you can go directly to dusting cabinet fronts without a second thought. At the start of this hour, put one load of laundry in the washer moving it to the dryer at the end of the hour.

Gather supplies:

- 10 soft cloths (enough for one kitchen and one bathroom cleaning)
- Scrub brush dedicated to kitchen use
- All-purpose cleaner that can handle grease
- All-purpose cleaner that can disinfect
- Scrub brush dedicated to bathroom use

Kitchen: Upper Cabinets and Shelves

There will be time for a deep clean of both the upper and lower cabinets, but in this hour, we're going to focus on the areas that receive a lot of use. Identify the upper cabinets and shelves that receive the bulk of the use in the kitchen. It may just be the range hood and the refrigerator (face and handles). It could also include the cabinet where everyday dishes are stored.

- Wipe them down with a soft cloth dampened with your favorite all-purpose cleaner that can tackle grease. You can also use a homemade vinegar recipe from the recipes chapter of this book.

Countertops:

Take the same cloth used for the upper cabinets and shelves and wipe down all of the counters.

1. Begin with a small open section where you can wipe front to back without encountering small appliances or other items stored on the counter.
2. Once this section is wiped of large debris with the same soft cloth, set it aside. You'll use it again in a minute
3. Get out a fresh soft cloth and your favorite countertop cleaner that can also disinfect.

4. Spray and wipe down the section of counter
5. To speed dry, you can use a third soft cloth to wipe down the counter
6. Move countertop items to the clean section of the counter to create a new pocket of countertop to clean
7. Start the process over. With the soft cloth used to wipe down upper cabinets and shelves, wipe off large debris from a section of the clear countertop
8. Set aside and grab your soft cloth and disinfectant cleaner
9. Use the third cloth for speed drying. Return the countertop items to where they were and move on to the next section.
10. Repeat this process until you've reached all of the countertops

Lower Cabinets and Shelves:

With a fresh soft cloth (we're up to 4 so far, more if you changed cloths during tasks as they dirty), grab your favorite all-purpose cleaner with degreaser to focus on high-use areas of cabinet fronts and shelves.

1. Examine the cabinet fronts below the sink, on both sides of the range, and near the garbage can.
2. After identifying the areas, clean them one by one changing out the cloth if it gets dirty

Sink:

If there are still dishes in your sink and you can't load them into the dishwasher or dish rack because they are also full, rinse them quickly and stack on the counter next to the sink. They will be a breeze to wash or load into the dishwasher when this hour is over. By putting them back in the sink after cleaning it, you'll be motivated to get them washed so you can enjoy the fruit of your labor.

After clearing the sink of dishes, grab a soft cloth and the all-purpose cleaner that can disinfect.

1. Start with the faucet and fixtures by spraying them, wiping them down and rinsing them with a second soft cloth that's been dampened and polishing dry with a third cloth
2. With the second soft cloth sprayed with all-purpose cleaner, wipe down the area between the backsplash and the edge of the sink, working your way around the base of the faucet and fixtures
3. Using your favorite sink cleaner, which could be the all-purpose cleaner that disinfects, spray down the sink. Using a plastic bristle brush or other appropriate tool to protect the surface of the sink, scrub in a circular motion getting the cleaner in every spot.
4. Rinse the sink with water. Replace any rinsed dishes and wipe down the part of the counter where they sat while you were cleaning the sink.

Bathroom:

In the bathroom, it's imperative to disinfect almost every surface. This can be done in a 7-day clean with a little strategy. Unlike the kitchen where you're working in a circular motion around the room in addition to focusing on specific areas, the bathroom requires attention only on one area at a time.

Vanity:

To speed up the process, take any products you had grouped together during the declutter day and move them to either the floor of the shower or a space in your bedroom. The top of a dresser or shelf with just enough space to hold everything works fine.

1. With a soft cloth and an all-purpose cleaner with disinfectant, spray down the mirror of the vanity avoiding streaks from too much cleaner sprayed at once.
2. Using the same soft cloth, begin wiping down the faucet, sink, and vanity top. Using the disinfectant all-purpose cleaner, focus on spots like dried toothpaste, water spots, and similar. Try to wipe up all of these leftover products in this soft cloth.

3. Put aside the soft cloth for laundering and grab a new one.
4. Spray faucet, sink, and vanity top once more with cleaner and wipe down with the new soft cloth.
5. Continuing downward, wipe down the front and side of the vanity. Include the base that meets the floor if you have a pedestal sink.
6. Return products to the vanity top

Shower:

Remove all products placing them in the bathroom sink, or if they're dry, on a surface nearby like a shelf or similar.

1. Spray down the shower walls with your favorite shower cleaner.
2. Using a scrub brush safe for your shower wall material, scrub in large circular motions working your way from one end of the shower to the other.
3. Spray the shower area once more.
4. Using a large soft cloth, wipe down the shower starting at one end and working your way around to the other.
5. Make sure you wipe down the showerhead and handle.
6. In the shower basin or tub, spray liberally with the shower cleaner.
7. Repeat the process of scrubbing in large circular motions before wiping down with a cloth.
8. Return products to their space in the shower area.

Toilet:

With a fresh soft cloth and disinfectant cleaner, spray and wipe the cover of the toilet tank before moving down to wiping the tank itself, including the lever.

1. Grab a new soft cloth and spray with cleaner before siping down the toilet seat cover, both sides of the toilet seat, and the top of the bowl itself.
2. Use the same disinfectant cleaner in the bowl itself or use your favorite toilet bowl cleaner to clean the toilet bowl.

3. With a new soft cloth, spray and wipe down the outside of the toilet bowl making sure you wipe the base

If you have more than one bathroom in your home, begin with the one that gets used most. After completing the kitchen and the first bathroom, there is often time in this hour to tackle a powder bathroom or a second full bathroom guests use. The key is to follow the steps in the order they're laid out, beginning with gathering the right supplies before beginning.

Day 3: Bedroom and Living Areas

With the exception of the laundry room, these spaces are dry meaning dusting will be at the top of the list in each one. In this hour, you'll be cleaning around the neat piles of items organized on Day 1 giving each surface the extra sparkle that comes from a good wipe down. The order of the rooms is important. Start with the bedroom and move on to the next largest living area, like your living room. Getting these large spaces out of the way allows you to sail through the rest of the smaller spaces wrapping up in the hour timeframe. Like with the other days, put a load of laundry in the washer at the start of the hour and move it to the dryer at the end of the hour.

Gather supplies:

- 8-10 soft cloths
- All-purpose cleaner safe for furniture surfaces
- All-purpose cleaner with disinfectant

Bedroom:

To speed up the process, leave your dry duster at home for the bedroom. Grab a soft cloth and spritz a little of your favorite all-purpose cleaner safe for furniture surfaces on it before getting started.

Wipe down furniture surfaces starting with the highest points, changing out cloths as they get dirty:

1. Top of the headboard
2. Tall dresser
3. Mirror
4. Lower dresser
5. Nightstand

Wipe down the mirror front with a fresh soft cloth and all-purpose cleaner. If you notice any dust buildup on the sides of furniture, go ahead and grab a fresh soft cloth spritzed with cleaner and wipe them down.

Living Area:

Starting with the taller hard surfaces, wipe down using a soft cloth dampened with all-purpose cleaner safe for the living area surfaces:

1. Top of fireplace mantle
2. Tops of accessory furniture (side tables, sideboards, coffee tables)
3. Top of TV and sound equipment
4. Bases of lamps
5. Bases of other furniture

Entryway or Mudroom:

1. Start with the door and door handle.
2. Take a fresh soft cloth and spritz with all-purpose cleaner before wiping down the door, focusing on the toe kick area and the area around the door handle.

3. Wipe down any window component of the entryway door.
4. With a fresh soft cloth, wipe down any shelves or cabinet fronts in the entryway area.

Laundry Room:

1. Starting with the tops of the machines or countertops, use a soft cloth dampened with water to wipe off detergent residue and large debris.
2. With a fresh cloth, spray disinfecting all-purpose cleaner and wipe these surfaces again.
3. Wipe down shelves or cabinet fronts by moving products to one side, cleaning, and then replacing the products as you move from shelf to shelf

If you have additional living areas like a home office or craft room, use the living area section to help you tackle it in this hour.

Day 4: Kitchen and Bathroom Floors

If you weren't careful with wiping the contents of your countertops into your hands on Day 2, then you're probably itching to get to this day. It's worth waiting for when at the end of this hour, you have not only sparkling floors, but counters you already cleaned. Gather your supplies and dive into this hour on your journey to a clean home in 7 days. Remember to start with your load of laundry.

Supplies:

- Vacuum
- Dry mop system (mop, 4 or more pads)
- Appropriate cleaners for the floor types
- 2-4 soft cloths

Kitchen:

1. Pick up any mats that cannot be vacuumed and shake outside.
2. Vacuum the floor before setting vacuum in bathroom.
3. Apply your preferred floor cleaner to any spots on the floor.
4. Wipe each spot with a soft cloth to completely remove it.
5. Use the dry mop system on the floor and change pads at least halfway through cleaning. This will prevent dragging dirt across the floor.
6. Replace floor mats.

Bathroom:

1. Pick up any bath mats and put them in the hamper for laundering.
2. Vacuum the floor.
3. Identify any spots and apply cleaner to wipe them up with a soft cloth.
4. Using the dry mop system, mop the floors using one pad for the area around the toilet and a new pad for the rest of the bathroom floor.
5. Replace bath mats with freshly cleaned ones, if available. If not, start a load with the bath mats removed

Floors tend to look simple on paper. There's basically two steps to cleaning them: vacuum and then mop. You will most likely finish both of these rooms in less than an hour. This allows you to tackle other bathrooms in your home bringing them up to the same level as your bathroom of initial focus.

Day 5: Living Areas

The dry mop system really comes into play when trying to clean the floors of the living areas in a reasonable amount of time. With the kitchen and bathroom, you most likely had the same type of cleaner in both rooms because they had the same floor material. In the living areas, it's common for the flooring material to go from carpet to hardwood to vinyl. This shouldn't scare you, however. Grab your supplies and make the most of this power hour. Start your load of laundry before you start this hour.

Supplies:

- A vacuum that can work on hard floor, as well as, carpet. Otherwise, two vacuums if you have separate machines for the two floor types
- Dry mop system
- 4-6 soft cloths

All Living Areas

To make this section easy to follow, everything is in one list. Follow it for each living area and omit any that don't apply to the room you're in.

1. Vacuum the area, working around any neatly grouped items like shoes by moving them to get to where they sit
2. For carpet, go back to any stains and spray with your favorite carpet cleaner according to the directions on the label.
3. If possible, let the cleaner sit while you move onto the next room setting a timer for the appropriate time to remind you to go back and finish the process.
4. For hard flooring, find any tough spots and spray with cleaner before wiping up with a soft cloth.
5. For hard flooring, use the dry mop system and change out pads frequently as you cover large expanses of flooring.
6. Move around groupings of belongings to reach the floor underneath.

Day 6: Windows

You may have felt the windows were being neglected earlier in the week. That's because they're one of the easiest cleaning tasks. However, their volume necessitates their own hour devoted to making them sparkle. Gather your supplies and start your load of laundry.

Supplies:

- Window cleaner, homemade or store bought
- 15-20 soft cloths
- Step stool (optional)

Start on the highest floor of your home working in a clockwise pattern around the level. With your soft cloth in hand, spray down your cloth with window cleaner before wiping the window panes in a circular motion. Spraying directly onto the cloth prevents cleaner from running down onto the trim of the window. Make sure you wipe into the corners of the glass to prevent spots of dust being left behind. If you use too much cleaner, use a dry soft cloth to wipe the window again in a circular motion dissolving the excess cleaner without leaving streaks.

Move to the next floor down before beginning the process again. If you notice the window sills need attention, don't worry, they're part of the deep cleaning list tackled in the next chapter.

Day 7: Laundry and Catch All

At this point, you're probably wondering why you did so many loads of laundry this week without even bothering to put everything away. You may have maxed out the number of containers you have to hold clean laundry and started living out of them for clothes needed for the day. Don't worry. There's a method here. In these loads of laundry, you should have cleaned your bath mats, bed sheets, clothes, and even towels. You might be using an old sheet set on your bed you don't really like and there's a hand towel acting as a mat in the bathroom, but the point is all your favorite linens are now clean. During this hour, put them all away. Lay out the bathmats on the still fresh floor you mopped on Day 4. Put your favorite sheets on your bed. Set up a folding command post on your bed where you can lovingly fold your clothes before putting them away.

This hour is also for catching up. You can take a few minutes to get all the shoes left in the living room or catch up on dishes in the sink. Use the time to suit you.

At the end of these 7 days, you'll be amazed at what you can accomplish when you take an hour out of each day to improve your home. This challenge isn't mean to take place everyday and indeed it can't. You have commitments in other areas of your life that require your time. The purpose of this challenge is to get your home to the point where it's easy to maintain. This base level of clean saves the frustration that comes with trying to just get started in a messy home. Now that you've completed the challenge, you don't have to worry about starting to clean the bathroom only to get distracted and unmotivated by the clutter. You're now set up for seamless cleaning time that is not wasted. By allotting hours this week for focused cleaning, you're giving your future self more time to do what you please.

Chapter 12: Maintenance & Monthly Habits

After completing the 7-day cleaning challenge, you should feel one step ahead in the care and maintenance of your home. It's not easy to dedicate an hour each day for 7 consecutive days to something like cleaning. There is work to be done, errands to be run, children and pets to care for. They all take your attention and cleaning falls to the bottom of the list. One of the greatest benefits of the challenge is that at the end, you're ready to go into full maintenance mode. It's a state of being that is less intense, requires less time, and is the glue that will keep your house together. Grab a coffee or tea and your calendar and let's begin putting together your maintenance schedule.

Follow the yearly calendar: With your calendar in hand, look over your commitments during the week, month, and course of the year.

It's impossible to predict every commitment in a 12-month span, but you can determine what times of the year are the busiest. December may be far off in the calendar at this moment, but you know there's at least one holiday party, a holiday craft bazaar, and other traditional gatherings. Knowing this, don't put anything on the deep cleaning list in December. You most likely won't get to it and feel defeated when January 1 rolls around with the task unfinished.

Follow the weather: If you live in a fair weather climate where each season offers ample opportunity to be outside, you can rely less on weather patterns and more on your own schedule. If you live in a climate with distinct seasons, including one that makes it impossible to complete work outside, you'll need to balance the weather's schedule with your own. Rather than starting with the fair weather seasons, take the coldest seasons and put together everything you can do during that time. This will keep you from feeling like the warmer months are overwhelmed with cleaning tasks.

Follow your average week: Look at a recent week in your schedule that was unusually busy. You may have had a different commitment every evening or more errands than usual to prep for a big trip. If so, then look at a week where things were slow. It may have been a week where you tried tackling cleaning the entire house on a Saturday because there was finally an open weekend on your calendar. Or maybe there were multiple nights where you were home by 6pm and got to veg out in front of the TV. Now, calculate the amount of time you dedicated to cleaning in each of those two weeks. Did you clean your bathroom and get your kitchen sparkling during the slow week? Was vacuuming the living area all you managed during the busy week? Take that amount of time and divide it by 7. That's your base amount of cleaning time for each day. Since you're looking to transform your home into better shape, add 10 minutes to that daily base of time. From there, decide where in your day that time fits best. If you're a morning person, you might want to take care of cleaning tasks before you start your day. If you get a second wind after dinner, section off that time and dedicate it to checking off the tasks on you list.

Now that you've figured out exactly how much time you can devote to your home each week, you must now decide what to do with it. Using the timed methods in previous chapters for each room, begin building your weekly time allotment with these tasks. Make sure you build in some time to catch up when weeks get busier than others.

For an example of a weekly cleaning schedule with monthly habits rolled in, I have provided the schedule for my own home. I live in a climate with four distinct seasons and have been able to carve out 20 minutes a day for housecleaning.

Weekly Schedule (Year-Round):

Monday:

- Start a load of laundry and move to dryer
- Kitchen: Wipe down counters
- Kitchen: Sweep

Tuesday:

- Fold laundry from Monday
- Bathroom: Wipe down vanity and sink
- Bathroom: Clean toilet
- Bathroom: Sweep
- Bathroom: Spray vinegar cleaner in shower to squeegee off after showering

Wednesday:

- Start a load of laundry and move to dryer
- Living areas: Dust and declutter
- Living areas: Vacuum

Thursday:

- Fold laundry from Wednesday
- Entryway/laundry room: Declutter and dust
- Entryway/laundry room: Vacuum

Friday:

- Start a load of bed sheets and move to dryer
- Bedroom: Declutter and dust
- Bedroom: Vacuum

Saturday (1 hour instead of 20 minutes):

- Make bed with clean sheets
- Vacuum floors and dry mop

Sunday:

- Rest
- Make a family dinner and use the cooking time to wipe down small appliances in the kitchen, reorganize the fridge and pantry for the week

I make small changes to my weekly schedule to accommodate for more or less mess in certain areas, but I try to keep the rooms the same each day. This helps to know exactly which room is touched on which day and saves me from wondering when a certain room is going to get some attention. Some days I have more than 20 minutes. I use that time for cleaning, but I don't try to hold myself to half an hour everyday when 20 will do a good enough job. This book is to help acquire the habit of cleaning without turning you into someone who spends all their free time with a scrub brush in hand.

Monthly Cleaning

January:

- Refrigerator and Freezer: After the holidays, the leftovers begin to hoard space in the fridge. Even if you don't get around to cleaning the refrigerator monthly, make sure January is a month that gets this task done.
- Indoor Plants: This is a bonus task for homes like mine that have many plants. It's a time I take to set old newspapers over a large swath of floor in my living room to revive each potted plant. I either re-pot it or mix in new, nutrient rich soil. When it's warmer outside, all my attention goes to my outdoor plants. The winter weather gives me the excuse to dote on the house plants that bring me joy and clean air.
- Holiday storage: Many people get excited about the holidays and the decorations that come with. The joy is multiplied 10x over from the work you can do in January when putting decorations

away. During this process, inspect decorations for any breaks or deficiencies before storing. Invest in sturdy storage bins that last and take time to properly label each bin. Once complete, everything is safe and easy to find when it's time to decorate again.

February:

- Oven: After holiday baking, give your oven a good cleaning with either your favorite oven cleaner or set the self-cleaning function.
- Baseboards: Take time to wipe down baseboards in all the rooms using soft cloths and an all-purpose cleaner safe for painted or sealed surfaces.
- Replace the home air filter.

March:

- Light fixtures: Take your time cleaning each component including the lamp shade, base, and even the cord. Start at the top of your house and work your way down.
- Clean appliances: Run the cleaning cycle on your washer and clean out the dryer ducts of lint. Clean vacuums and their filters. Run a cleaning cycle on your dishwasher.

April:

- Clothes closets: When I'm already swapping out my wardrobe with the impending season change from cold to warm, I like to take all of my clothes out of the closet and dresser. I inspect each piece for defects and assess if I want to continue holding onto it. I donate what I don't keep and my closet looks fresh from decreasing the stock.
- Clean refrigerator and freezer: Make room for all the new produce showing up at your local farmer's market by repeating this task from January. Remove all food, wipe interior, wash shelves, and replace everything.

May:

- Windows: Wash the interior of all the windows in your home. Then, at the same time or a later date, clean the sills of all the built-up dirt, dead bugs, and dust.
- Outdoor Living: Set up the outdoor living area for warmer weather by bringing furniture and cushions out of storage. Sweep the area and wipe down furniture to clear the dust.

June:

- Replace the home air filter
- Window treatments: Launder or dust off window treatments throughout your home.
- Bedding: On a hot sunny day, lay out pillows and bedding like down comforters to naturally deodorize them and kill dust mites.

July:

- Baseboards: Give them a quick clean using your vacuum and the brush attachment
- Upholstery: Look over upholstered furniture for any spots and treat them with a fabric cleaner. Launder, if necessary.

August:

- Refrigerator and freezer: Before you even see holiday decorations in stores, clean out your fridge and freezer so they're ready for the holidays ahead.

September:

- Windows: Clean the interior of your windows one more time before cooler weather arrives.
- Windows: Take time and wash the exterior of all your windows to keep them sparkling through the colder months.

October:

- Garage: Take advantage of cooler temperatures to get some heavy-lifting done in the garage. Get rid of unused equipment, reorganize the storage, and sweep out the floor before putting everything back.
- Replace the home air filter

November:

- Declutter: Spend 20 minutes in each room of the house decluttering. Take unused items to be donated or consigned. Put back everything you're keeping in an organized manner. Return items that belong in other rooms in your home. This will get you ready for holiday decorating and gatherings.
- Clean appliances: Run another cleaning cycle on appliances like washers and dishwashers. Clean out the dryer duct of excess lint. Clean your vacuum.

December:

- Don't schedule any deep cleans this month if you have a lot of seasonal events.

Considering what's possible to accomplish each month of the year, you've got this. You can make a schedule that not only maintains a clean home, but keeps stress and worry away. I included the weekly cleaning list with the year-long monthly tasks because they're interlocked in their mission to keep your home spotless. They work together to avoid instances where you're spending your entire Saturday deep cleaning every part of the house because you can't remember the last time you did. With a monthly and weekly schedule, you can feel confident that every inch of your home is covered over the course of a year.

You'll notice December is blocked off from deep cleaning tasks to give yourself time for the holiday season. If December isn't that busy of a month for you, move that deep clean-free time somewhere else. Maybe you need a break in January or the middle of summer because that's when your family travels. Determine when that is and schedule it in. Give yourself a break at some point in the year to avoid burnout. It's so easy to let something as simple as cleaning get in the way of happiness and contentment. Get ahead of it and don't let it steal any more attention than it needs.

This schedule you're building for yourself will take from the rest of this book. The timed tasks and methods for cleaning each area will come together piece by piece. You'll build it according to the time you have to devote to each task. You'll also have various factors that impact how your schedule is made. If you have a robotic vacuum, your cleaning time will be devoted to preparing the area for it to run. If you have a monthly cleaning service that can help with larger deep clean projects, you'll spend less of your Saturday wiping windows or the like.

The monthly schedule is especially helpful for vacation rentals. It's not always easy to plan when a deep clean project can get done. However, if you know that in a certain month certain tasks should be completed, you can work them into your schedule around check-ins and check-outs.

To help build your weekly schedule, I've included a chart of tasks and the time they take. Gathering all the information from other chapters and adding it here will help you get started on building a schedule. You can always refer to the other chapters for more cleaning techniques and product suggestions. The following chart is your quick reference when you need it.

	10 minute tasks	20 minute tasks	30 minute tasks
Kitchen	• Declutter counters • Wipe down appliances	• Unload and load the dishwasher and/or dishrack • Sweep and mop floors	• Clear the counters • Clean inside appliances
Bathroom	• Clear surfaces • Wipe down surfaces	• Sweep and mop floors • Focus on sinks and toilets	• Dust surfaces like towel bars and shelves • Grout cleaning (up to 45 minutes)
Bedroom	• Make bed • Fold laundry	• Vacuum floors • Clear clutter	• Wipe down surfaces • Return items that belong in other rooms

	10 minute tasks	20 minute tasks	30 minute tasks
Living Area	• Clear surfaces • Dust surfaces	• Sweep or vacuum floors • Dry mop floors	• Return items that belong in other rooms • Wipe down furniture and spot clean upholstery
Other Areas	• Clear surfaces • Dust surfaces	• Sweep or vacuum floors • Dry mop floors	• Return items that belong in other rooms • Wipe down surfaces like doors in entryways, machines in laundry room, etc.

Most people are surprised by the amount of time they spend on cleaning each week, trying to make their house look a certain way. However, the time spent does not create the desired result. By taking that time and adding a little bit more where needed, you can work smarter, not harder to have a sparkling home. Once you've completed the 7-day cleaning challenge, the next task is implementing your new schedule. The first week will tell you everything you need to know about adjustments and improvements. Refer back to this chapter as you hone your schedule and find everything you need to boost your success.

Conclusion

You've reached the end of this book but the beginning of a new era in your home. Depending on your reading style you might have read the book cover to cover over the course of a few days. Alternatively, you might have read up to the 7-day cleaning challenge, started that, and came back to finish the rest. However you consumed this book, I hope it has changed how you see cleaning in your home. At the start of this book, you might not have known the wonders of a dry mop system and your clutter was taking over your life, as well as any free time you had on Saturdays.

Cleaning was not just a chore for you, but something you dreaded. An inescapable fact of life that you swore was out to get you. You might have tried to get your act together and find a cleaning system to work for you. This could be your first or 50th attempt at incorporating a solid cleaning game plan into your schedule. You picked up this book and with another deep breath, dove in. You took the first steps on a new journey and the pages within showed you the rest of the way. I promised you a fresh start and with each chapter, showed you the way.

Starting with tried and tested cleaning recipes, this book brought to you a new depth of knowledge when it comes to cleaning your home. There are many uses for everyday products sitting in cabinets and pantries. With the right combination, you can find the product needed to tackle any cleaning job in your home. Sometimes the mess has gotten out of hand. You inherited a dingy bathroom when moving into your new apartment or the space you want to become a vacation rental looks more like a vacation nightmare. To restore your space to a spotless clean you can maintain were lists of products to get the job done right.

As with the cleaning recipes and favorite tools, each room was scrutinized for the best way to deep clean and then maintain. The focus on deep cleaning techniques paired with their maintenance cousins was to battle every roadblock that's ever stopped you from cleaning before.

Whether it was being overwhelmed by the scope of the cleaning needed, or life getting in the way of a cleaning schedule you made. Your motivation wanes. Your space descends further into chaos with your attempts to restore your home to clean thrown in.

By sharing deep cleaning methods marked with the time they take to complete, this book empowers you to tackle everything in your home. To show you that's possible, the 7-day cleaning challenge brought you together with method of cleaning to bring your home into balance. By comparing your home at the beginning of the challenge and the end, you see firsthand what you're capable of accomplishing. Any previous attempts at maintaining a clean home wash away from memory. You're in the here and now.

A cleaning challenge wasn't enough, however. You needed to find a way to clean your home in the time already available to you during the week. You needed to work smarter and not harder in the time you were already giving to your home. By sitting down and assessing how much time that is, you were able to take the tasks and times given for each room and make a cleaning schedule that works for you.

You've found the motivation to not only clean, but to open up your space to support the life you want to live. The vacation rental you've been wanting to get started is in sight now. The dream of hosting friends and family more regularly looks like a reality. In each room, the motivation builds as you arm yourself with new techniques and tricks to keep clutter at bay and the space cleaner for longer.

In each room, you now have the tools and products needed to keep the space clean. Your focus is no longer scattered, but set precisely on different tasks based on the time they take. As you refer back to this book again and again, you'll find more of it sticking with you. As it sets in your mind, cleaning will become not only a task to be completed but an accomplishment you look forward to reaching. You'll love the way it feels to know exactly what needs to be done in each room and when.

Living rooms can be lived in and still look chic for a gathering of friends. Kitchens are always ready for cooking because of a few minutes spent strategically decluttering. Bathrooms are prepared for guests at any moment saving you any embarrassment. Entryways and mudrooms can not only take the clutter of shoes and coats, but look good doing it. Questions about "Does this need to be cleaned?" have been answered and guided steps given to achieve that clean.

Rather than spend hours on a Saturday or try to meet some arbitrary daily goal of cleaning, you sat down with your schedule and found space that already existed. You transformed the time you already spent on cleaning into time that's efficient. The time dedicated to cleaning in your schedule is satisfying because you see the end in sight. You know that when you spend an hour on a space, you're going to accomplish x, y, and z.

Instead of bouncing around to different deep cleaning tasks done in times of panic and crisis, you're already plotting out the future. You've learned to take the seasons of your life throughout the year and maximize your time with different deep cleans in different months. No more smoking ovens at the holidays because you forgot the last time you cleaned the oven. No more stuffy house in winter because it's too cold to be outside. You know exactly what needs to be done and when.

The other key points to keep in mind include:

- Look in your cabinets. Use household supplies you already have to make cleaning products.
- Find your starting point. In every room, no matter the task, there's a starting point to help you get off on the right foot and finish the tasks at hand. Whether it's working clockwise around the room, starting at the top and working your way down, or sometimes a combination of both.

- Find the right tools. From surface to surface, room to room, make sure you're arming yourself with the tools to make each cleaning task go smoothly.
- Both deep cleaning and maintenance cleaning work together to help make your home sparkle.
- Take the 7-day challenge. By dedicating an hour each day to cleaning, you can take your home from overwhelming to being ready for anything.
- Revamp your time spent on housecleaning with a schedule that combines deep cleaning tasks with maintenance ones.

All of the knowledge put forth in this book comes from years of research and lived experience. I wanted to feel in power within my home and I wanted to feel in charge when it came time to open a vacation rental. I spent countless hours and dollars trying new cleaning products and honing my must-have list to tackle anything my house threw at me. I knew long ago I didn't want to keep it all with me. I wanted to share it with others and empower them to take control of their spaces.

You have that knowledge now and thus the power to take control of your space. If there's one thing I want you to take away from this book, it's that statement. You are empowered with knowledge that can overcome any anxiety you had around cleaning. There may have been a million attempts on your part to find a cleaning solution that stuck, but this book is the last one for you. It's here to help you in every step of your cleaning journey and stay with you like a favorite cookbook. It's a reference for everything going forward and a reminder of what you can do no matter your space. Use it well and find the balance of clean that makes you feel at home.

Bibliography

Saxbe, D. E., & Repetti, R. (2009). No Place Like Home: Home Tours Correlate With Daily Patterns of Mood and Cortisol. *Personality and Social Psychology Bulletin, 36*(1), 71–81. https://doi.org/10.1177/0146167209352864

Florida State University. (2015, October 1). Chore or stress reliever: Study suggests that washing dishes decreases stress. *ScienceDaily.* Retrieved December 11, 2019 from www.sciencedaily.com/releases/2015/10/151001165852.htm